How to Think about Politics

T0383977

How to Think about Politics

Politics

A Guide in Five Parts

PETER ALLEN

OXFORD
UNIVERSITY PRESS

Oxford University Press is a department of the University of Oxford.
It furthers the University's objective of excellence in research, scholarship,
and education by publishing worldwide. Oxford is a registered trade mark of
Oxford University Press in the UK and in certain other countries.

Published in the United States of America by Oxford University Press
198 Madison Avenue, New York, NY 10016, United States of America.

Library of Congress Cataloging-in-Publication Data
Names: Allen, Peter (Political scientist), author.
Title: How to think about politics : a guide in five parts / Peter Allen.
Description: New York, NY : Oxford University Press, [2025] |
Includes bibliographical references and index.|
Identifiers: LCCN 2024046261 (print) | LCCN 2024046262 (ebook) |
ISBN 9780197679364 (pbk) | ISBN 9780197679357 (hbk) |
ISBN 9780197679388 (epub) | ISBN 9780197679395
Subjects: LCSH: Political science.
Classification: LCC JA71 .A4746 2025 (print) | LCC JA71
(ebook) | DDC 320—dc23/eng/20241205
LC record available at https://lccn.loc.gov/2024046261
LC ebook record available at https://lccn.loc.gov/2024046262

DOI: 10.1093/9780197679395.001.0001

Paperback printed by Integrated Books International, United States of America
Hardback printed by Bridgeport National Bindery, Inc., United States of America

MIX
Paper
FSC FSC® C183721

For my parents, Angela and Tony

Can we graciously disagree?
I am tired of people

not knowing the volume
of their power. Who doesn't

deserve
some silence at night?

Raymond Antrobus, excerpt from *The Rebellious*[1]

Contents

Acknowledgments

Matthew Barnfield and Neil Matthews have read almost every word of this, something for which I am deeply grateful. Thanks to Brad Clark, who helped hone the initial idea and proposal. For other comments and conversations I would like to thank Patrick Bury, Jack Copley, Ivan Gololobov, Sophia Hatzisavvidou, Andrew Hindmoor, Mauro Lubrano, David S. Moon, Deivi Norberg, Karl Pike, Liam Stanley, and Kateřina Vráblíková.

Thanks to Nick Pearce and the University of Bath's Institute for Policy Research for facilitating the sabbatical leave that allowed me to finish the book. Thanks again to Sophia Hatzisavvidou for taking over my duties as our Department's Director of Research while I was on leave, a gift that gave me the space to get this thing done.

At OUP, thanks to Emily Benitez, Mhairi Bennett, and Dave McBride for all of their help. Thanks to Rajeswari Azayecoche for managing production and thanks to Anne Sanow for her meticulous copyediting of the text.

Thanks to Fiona, Daniel, Erin, Cormac, and Fenny. Special thanks to Charlotte, my system for everything. Finally, thanks to my parents, Angela and Tony, to whom this book is dedicated.

Peter Allen
Bristol
September 2024

Introduction
Breathe the Air

The Fundamentals

I was nine years old when Tony Blair led the center-left Labour Party to a landslide victory at the 1997 UK general election. Waking up on Friday, May 2, I spoke to my grandmother on the phone, who instructed me, for what would be the first time in my life, to "go outside and breathe Labour air." That morning, I was given the idea that politics could change things a lot and quickly—it sounded like something worth paying attention to.

Air is all around us. We breathe it in and breathe it out, all the time. And although air can vary depending on where you are—some air more polluted, some more fresh—ultimately it is the same air everywhere. As the smoke-filled air caused by a Californian wildfire crossing a country to New York City, then crossing the ocean to me here in the UK shows us, we are all in this particular thing together. And we breathe in and breathe out without really thinking about it. We just breathe; this is how it is. Unless we are meditating or undertaking some other breathing practice that focuses our mind on the process, the whole thing happens without our input. We only notice it when we choose to or—of course—when it goes wrong. We generally aren't aware of it but it shapes our life; it *is* our life. Most of the time, for most people, politics too operates in the background while affecting us all nonetheless. It's everywhere, in and out of everything, all the time, whether we are aware of it or not.

I was born toward the end of the 1980s, growing up in the suburbs of Greater London. While I cannot discount the rosy tint

How to Think about Politics. Peter Allen, Oxford University Press. © Oxford University Press (2025).
DOI: 10.1093/9780197679395.003.0001

that the stress-free nature of childhood generally imparts on such reminiscences, it did feel like people around my age had a pretty good run of things for the decade and a half that followed. In fact, depending on how you looked at things, you could even extend this window of relative calm to around 2008, the year that the global financial crisis took hold. For those fifteen to twenty years political parties seemed to argue about how to make things better, not about which version of things getting worse they would prefer to implement and some of the grimmest legacies of the twentieth century appeared to be destined to remain in the past, certainly no longer acceptable in mainstream politics.

It was thus with a sense of optimism that I began studying politics, first at school, then at university, initially as a student before teaching it to others as a lecturer, something I've now done for over a decade. For much of this period, I was positive about politics and those who were involved in it—bumps in the road were just that, bumps on an otherwise reasonably smooth surface. Bad apples were bad apples—unfortunate deviations, sure, but in the broad sweep of things, I was able to keep faith with my positive story about politics and what it could achieve. All told, to my younger self it felt like a time of things opening up, not closing in. This was a naive feeling, perhaps, but it was a real one all the same.

It wouldn't last. By late 2019, a friend and I were sitting at the bar in a small pub close to where I live in Bristol, and Donald Trump, a cartoonish reality TV star, was the president of the United States while Boris Johnson, an archetypal clown, was prime minister of the United Kingdom.[1] The river of problems flowing through political life—the climate crisis, the threat of nuclear war, the chronic degradation of democratic institutions—had burst its banks and politicians seemed, dangerously, to be urging the flow to speed up. My positive story about the capacity and potential of politics and politicians in tatters, this friend turned to me and asked, "If all these terrible things are happening, and politics is such a mess, what are people like you doing to fix it?" By people like me, she meant someone whose job it is to think, write, and teach others about politics. My initial reaction was to duck and cover and, in classic academic fashion, I displaced, deflected ("nobody listens," "we already are"). But I ultimately didn't interpret the inquiry as an accusation. Reflection on my part made me see that rather than a fleeting query, it was actually a much bigger question that deserved a proper response. This book is that response.

I started but did not finish this book during the COVID-19 pandemic. Although in theory I was one of those people who suddenly had more free time during the copious lockdowns—no caring responsibilities, the ability to work from home throughout, and nowhere to go—the reality was somewhat different. Doing work of any kind was hard. The pandemic was exhausting, strange, sad, funny, and rewarding. In other words, a microcosm of life itself, but a life restricted to my apartment and the couple of miles around it plus the odd dash to London once restrictions permitted. So while it isn't a book completed during COVID, it is a "COVID book" all the same in the sense that the events leading up to and including what we might think of as the "COVID era" have ultimately led me to think differently about my job and the subject I study and teach others about. It has made me dwell on the question of what people like me are doing at this time of political turbulence. It has also made me want to write something more personal, something that was curious and open to the possibility that despite apparently being an expert on a topic, maybe I didn't know that much after all. It made me want to take a step away from what I thought I already knew for certain, to revisit the fundamentals of this thing—politics—that I have spent my adult life thinking about.

It can be easy to feel overwhelmed by politics. It is a huge subject, leaving its imprint on essentially every aspect of our world. On top of this, we are also living through the most fitful political situation that most of us can remember. Norms are shattering, assumptions long taken for granted have been undermined, and events are moving so fast that even if you wanted to, it is hard to keep on top of it

4 HOW TO THINK ABOUT POLITICS

all. At a time when it feels that we really need to grasp what is going on, it is getting progressively harder to do so, a situation not helped by the seeming obsession with trivia among the media tasked with telling the rest of us about the political world. But allow me to let you in on a secret. It's not that hard to know quite a lot about politics. I don't mean the names and numbers and who did what—I'm not sure that kind of thing matters and, if it does, it doesn't matter much. What I mean are the fundamentals: the things that outlast the current Speaker of the House, a notorious newspaper political editor, or the latest opinion poll. I mean the things that are rooted in your life. My life. Our life, the one we all take part in on a daily basis. Maybe, then, we should stop trying to keep up and instead pause and step back. Think bigger. Think deeper. Rather than repeatedly getting caught in the swirl of day-to-day politics, maybe there is value in returning to the fundamentals and cultivating a set of tools and perspectives that can help us to interpret what we see going on around us. That's what I hope that this book will help you to do.

When Is Everything Going to Get Back to Normal?

In Season 5, Episode 3 of *Mad Men*, Roger Sterling, one of the partners of the advertising firm at the center of the show asks a question—"When is everything going to get back to normal?"— in response to the changes that the company is going through following a takeover by a larger outfit.[2] Rewatching the show in the last twelve months I was struck by how, in the face of a pandemic, climate change, and war following the invasion of a Western democracy by a neighbor, maybe all of us were too asking this question. Things do not feel normal right now. The historian Adam Tooze has popularized the term "polycrisis" to describe the multiple contemporary interlocking threats faced by the planet and those of us on it.[3] These can be characterized in various ways, but most accounts of the polycrisis focus on climate change, political instability, geopolitical conflict, and issues relating to economic growth or its opposite. Perhaps the trickiest part of the polycrisis is the extent to which these problems are melded together: like a Rubik's cube, if you fiddle with one side in an attempt to solve it, you simultaneously make your task more complicated when you turn over and start work on the other side. The polycrisis thus presents politicians and policymakers with numerous cases of what would historically have been once-in-a-generation problems at the same time.

And it isn't just the politicians who are in this position. Collectively, all of us have been forced to take a step away from certainty in the last decade and a half as the economic, political, and ecological conditions we took for granted (at least those of us living in advanced democracies) have been rocked. We might have to endure a summer in an unbearably hot city, pay more for our mortgage or rent, or be unable to travel to see friends and family owing to the repercussions of an ongoing war. These intersecting crises often take on an almost apocalyptic feel, with overwhelming wildfires accompanying the threat of nuclear war alongside turmoil in the financial markets. Writing about this in the context of the COVID-19 pandemic, the novelist Brandon Taylor reflected on how "the apocalypse is a kind of mass cultural event, an extinction in which each of us is queasily perched between the roles of observer and participant."[4] In politics, whether we see ourselves as "political" or not, we are already in this position and always will be—involved and watching, watching and involved.

Many, including me in other places, make the argument that we need more of us—more of you—to become engaged and involved in politics. We need to move people from just watching to doing. Achieving this, we think, would be a good thing all around. We would see a greater variety of life experience better represented in politics, we would more effectively hold our leaders to account for their actions and, maybe, we would see ourselves and each other differently, more fairly. But more and more I worry about relying on greater participation and engagement as the remedy to our ills. The situation we are actually in—where people have to work long hours, sometimes in multiple jobs, just to get by; where our news media is nowhere close to being equal to the task of reporting on political events; and where time is, frankly, running out on key issues like climate change—is not a situation conducive to a sudden uptick in political engagement.

Without suggesting that people shouldn't get involved in politics if they want to (they still should!), a different approach is nonetheless worth considering. For a while now I have been having the same persistent thought: people are already deeply immersed in politics in manifold ways. Even if they are not members of political parties or are not political news junkies, politics affects how their lives go. It affects their health, their happiness, and the health and happiness of everybody they love. Acknowledging this fact leads to a second, related thought: rather than trying to convert this immersion into a more recognizable form of political action, I think there may instead be hope in improving the quality of this already-existing engagement with all things political. It is possible to think more systematically about what we encounter, to ask better questions, and more clearly articulate our desires. We are already involved, like it or not! The raw material is there for the shaping.

Caring But Not Liking

Despite spending a lot of my life thinking about it, I don't really like politics. At least, I don't like politics if, by politics, we mean who is up and who is down at Westminster or in DC or what some new opinion poll says about whether or not a given politician is popular in the Rust Belt or wherever. I don't enjoy elections. I don't particularly like political news. But even though I don't like it, I nonetheless in some sense care about it. I think many of us are in this conflicted position—caring but not liking. My guess is that without realizing it, many of us care far more than we would consciously admit to, but this care does not translate into any kind of deeper reflection. It goes unacknowledged.

Being a professional student of politics—a political scientist—often results in people assuming that you have some privileged insight into the future direction of political events. Although this ability would indeed be a boon for my finances if successfully put to the test at a bookies, I can exclusively reveal to you that it is not the case. If one can actually "know more" about politics, this knowledge almost certainly does not result in being able to guess what happens next. Sure, there are a series of facts that one could learn about institutions, individuals, and states: how legislative bodies work; which politician is friends with another politician and what that might mean for their career prospects; or why some countries descend into civil conflict while others do not. But where would these facts leave us? Knowledgeable in some sense of the word, I accept, but I am not sure that this kind of knowledge is particularly relevant to how most of us experience politics in our daily lives.

Political science, the systematic empirical study of political phenomena, is good at addressing increasingly specific questions about why certain events and happenings come to pass and at offering some sort of explanation of how this happens. Political science tries to stand outside of politics and look at it from above (it is, after all, trying to be scientific). But we are not outside of politics, quite the opposite. We are in the middle of it all the time. Consequently, what political science has been less good at is giving us much of an idea of what we, as individuals, can do to both interpret these events and happenings and to talk about them in a more constructive and fruitful way. This book is my attempt to do exactly this—to offer readers a guide that, while rooted in lessons from political science and political theory, is focused on giving a sense of how you can interpret and discuss politics with greater confidence. Citizens who can discuss political events with confidence are, in all likelihood, less likely to simply parrot lines fed to them by opportunists. They are more likely to be able to articulate political demands for themselves, demands relating to issues they face in their own lives. They are more likely to hold the powerful to account but to also acknowledge politicians doing good when they see it. So think of the book as a sort of self-help guide not for your health, finances, or romantic life, but for your engagement with the political world.

I am not going to tell you *what* to think about politics. To do so would be, to a great extent, pointless and, as we are all painfully aware, there are enough voices already taking on that particular role. Instead, I want to direct your *attention* to certain things; I want to show you what I think is a series of good *processes* for thinking about politics. I make no presupposition regarding where you will end up. You may go along with me and redirect your attention onto some of the areas I discuss but come to a different conclusion about the implications of what you see. In other words, your idea as to what *should* come next might be completely different to my own. This, of course, is the nature of politics.

What Is to Come

The book focuses on what I see as the fundamentals of the subject I study: five political ideas, each discussed over the course of a chapter. These ideas are power, knowledge, presence, the question of what we want, and possibility. Why these ideas? The simple answer is that having spent almost half my life studying, teaching, and writing about politics, these ideas are the ones that I keep coming back to. More or less everything that happens in political life involves one, several, or all of them, something I will demonstrate across the course of the book.

The first idea is power. There is a story commonly told about power, namely that power flows through political institutions that exist to ensure it is used in a certain way by certain people. We expect power to turn up in a suit, behind a podium, cheered on by supporters. But is this the only kind of power? From our own lives we know that power comes in other, less visible, forms. There is power that operates largely in the background of societies, unelected and not invested in specific roles or offices, power that swishes around our most intimate relationships, and power that we encounter in the workplace as we are told what we can do and when. It is this tension between visible power and less visible power, the question of how we control these different kinds of power, and what this means for the way our societies work that this chapter is about. Power is about enforcing the rules of the game but it is also about writing them in the first place. It isn't just a question of what things we can do, but about the environment we do them in. Power is, to a great degree, everything in politics.

The second idea is knowledge. The dominant story about political knowledge is that most people don't have it. Not only this, the story also has it that people don't even want such knowledge: given the opportunity to change, they wouldn't. This story is wrong— or, at least, it isn't quite right. People do have political knowledge and they have it in abundance. The problem is that political scientists and politicians have been looking for the wrong thing and looking for it in the wrong places. What counts as political knowledge and, relatedly, who gets to decide this? The risk in proscribing what political knowledge is in a limited way consists in the influence this can subsequently have on ideas about when we should take someone's views on politics seriously—it sets political knowledge up as a test that can be passed or failed. And if this test judges only a selected few to be in possession of the relevant credentials, this may result in an assumption that we can listen to just these people and ignore everyone else. But rather than simply accepting the dominant story, political scientists have begun to consider alternative means of conceptualizing and measuring political knowledge, focusing on peoples' knowledge of their daily lives and experiences.

Measuring political knowledge in this way has highlighted that people have knowledge that differs by sex, class, and race. Rather than some people knowing a lot about politics and the rest of us not knowing much at all, on this view, we might all have something to offer.

Next up is presence. It has been possible to tell a good news story about political representation over recent decades as our elected leaders have become more diverse on just about every measure. More women, ethnic minorities, and LGBT+ legislators are now present in politics than ever before. But the good news story isn't the only story. The reality is that the wider impact of many of these advances in presence has been, to many, something of a disappointment. We may have had the first Black president of the US, the first British-Asian and the second (and, fleetingly, third) woman prime minister of the UK, but while these are clear gains for the diversity of political representation in one sense, the kinds of political transformations that some might have expected these previously inconceivable events to bring about have not materialized. Indeed, in some respects, things have gotten worse. The 2016 election of Donald Trump saw an outright sexist enter the most powerful office in the world even after the exposure of his comments about grabbing women "by the pussy" and globally, the rise of far-right political parties has led to a backlash against progressive policies that had broadly expanded or secured the rights of women, LGBT+ persons, ethnic minorities, and others who had historically been marginalized in political life. How can we understand these two concurrent but conflicting trends? This chapter confronts the limitations of presence in an age of polarization and increasing political complexity, arguing that political representation, while hugely important, is subject to significant constraints on what it can achieve. As such, if we put too much faith in the power of presence to change the world around us, we may be setting ourselves up for disappointment. We need to think carefully about what presence can do, what it can't, and, crucially, why.

Following this is the question of what we want. There were a few hundred people who followed Donald Trump around the United States, attending as many of his rallies as they could, and becoming friends with others who did the same—the "Front Row Joes"—in the process. These people were not wealthy (Trump winning the election would likely not benefit them in any tangible financial way). They also gave up a lot to commit to attending these rallies, including money, relationships with their families, and their time. The Front Row Joes prompt us to consider two things. First, they appeared to endorse something that seems, in a reasonably clear way, to not be good for them. Their support for a candidate who didn't seem to have any plans to actually do anything to help them complicates the basic assumption that voters would support and vote for political candidates and movements that would give them what they want—and that what they want will be material gains. Second, the Front Row Joes have made their political commitments an outsize part of their lives, certainly compared to the average person, something that should make us ponder whether the size and intensity of this commitment is right for them and the lives that on reflection, they might want to live. Thus, two questions shape this chapter: first, what should you want *out of* politics and, second, what do you want politics *to be* in your life? Politics is often seen as something separate from the rest of our lives. But whether we see ourselves as highly politically engaged or not, when we make the political choices that we are able to, limited as these might be, these choices are nonetheless very much about who we are as people and what we value in our lives. As such, our political choices should (and will) reflect who we are, and at the same time, who we are is in part constituted by our political choices. Politics goes all the way down. Thinking about these things together makes sense and, if you are looking for a more useful way to think about politics, you could do a lot worse than starting by trying to think in a more useful way about yourself—about what you value and what you want.

The final idea is possibility. Some physicists argue that if we accept certain theories of cosmic inflation—the idea that space is constantly expanding in size—we by implication accept the possible existence of parallel universes across a vast multiverse. Proponents of the multiverse idea argue that rather than what we consider to be the universal laws of physics remaining constant across all of the parallel universes, these laws may instead differ depending on which part of the multiverse a given universe exists within: the dials on the laws of physics are set at different points depending on where a universe is within the multiverse. The dials being adjusted in these cases may include dark-energy density, electron mass, and the dimensions of space and time. By comparison, in politics we generally aren't attempting to manipulate such heady stuff. In almost all cases, we are trying to change things that are already within our control, and usually in a reasonably modest fashion. Not only do the relevant dials actually exist; we already have the means to control them. Put another way, we already live in a political multiverse and if anybody is setting the dials, it is us. We do this on a daily basis through the stories we tell and the stories we accept about how things are and how they could be. We regularly end up doing the thing we thought was impossible, often suddenly and unexpectedly. Such actions tell us something about the fundamentally uncertain state of politics and the underlying possibility this presents—the boundaries are there for us to change if we want to. But we often don't do those things even though we could; something is framed as inevitable and it doesn't occur. Why? This chapter shows how the stories we tell about the world are powerful. They guide our actions and they shape our lives. Stories are arguments that the world is, can be, and will be, a certain way. Stories matter—they tell us what is possible and what is inevitable. But if we can look through one, think past it, see around it, we can see that a story is, ultimately, just that: a story. With sufficient will, we can tell a different one.

The book ends by bringing the five ideas to bear on the very real political problems presented by the polycrisis. Considering the interaction of the environmental, geopolitical, and economic crises that characterize the current political moment, the chapter demonstrates how we can use the five fundamental ideas discussed in the book to think about the different aspects of these problems. What can they illuminate?

A brief note on style—this book will be rooted in the arguments and evidence of the discipline of political studies, but will be written in a manner that I hope makes it accessible to just about anyone who wishes to read it. That is, no endless references to academic work, no unexplained technical terms, and no tedious debates about minutely different definitions of words or concepts. The five ideas are illustrated and discussed through examples from ongoing political events and popular culture including television and literature. While I do discuss examples from the United States, I betray my parochiality and often focus on the case of the United Kingdom. When I do so, I explain who and what the main moving parts of any example are. Further details will be provided in a notes section at the end of the book.

The Wisdom of Pausing

Like many people, my formative exposure to the political world was via the breathless coverage of contemporary events that epitomizes the way politics is spoken about most of the time. In addition to being the introduction to politics that is most common, it is also, unfortunately, for most as far as their engagement with politics goes. There is no next step, no moving beyond the noise and the chaos. For those of you reading this, however, I hope that what follows constitutes such a move.

There is a Buddhist idea of the wisdom of the pause—when we feel that we are caught in some moment, some intense experience, the best thing we can do is stop and wait before proceeding. This gives us time to think about how we actually feel. Do we need to carry on feeling how we did? Were we thinking clearly? Can we proceed in a different direction following this short break? This book, I hope, gives you a chance to pause and, in turn, tap into the wisdom that, underneath the chaos of contemporary politics, you already possess. This chaos isn't the most interesting part of politics and it's also not the most important. The fundamentals are.

How do we confront a political moment like the one we are in, this polycrisis? Honestly, I'm not certain of the answer. But what I am certain of is that whatever good eventually comes out of the current malaise, it will be the result of more people being engaged in thinking about politics in ways that emphasize these longstanding fundamentals over the swirling, evanescent mess of the present.

1

Think About Power

Holding the Ball

In June 2020, protesters who were part of a Black Lives Matter (BLM) gathering pulled down the statue of slave trader and philanthropist, Edward Colston, that stood in the center of Bristol, a city in the southwest of England. Then, they dragged the statue roughly 300 meters to the edge of Bristol harbor and heaved the statue over metal railings and into the water. The protest was peaceful and antagonism toward the police from the protesters, and vice versa, was minimal. In the days that followed, despite opinion polls showing apparent public support for the action in a general sense, there were what are by now perhaps some predictable reactions. Some right-of-center tabloids, echoed by the Conservative Home Secretary, Priti Patel, called for the "full force of the law" to be felt by those involved. This sentiment was repeated by others, including one prominent political scientist who on Twitter variously described the protestors at various BLM events as "an authoritarian group-based mob" who were "running amok."[1] Less strident, but in some ways more revealing, was the response of Keir Starmer, the then-reasonably recently elected Leader of the opposition Labour Party. Although Starmer agreed that the statue "should have been brought down a long time . . . ago," he added that "it shouldn't be done in that way, completely wrong to pull a statue down like that . . . that statue should have been brought down properly with consent and put, I would say, in a museum."[2] The insinuation here is clear—those who removed and submerged the statue were, in doing so, displaying power. They were powerful.

How to Think about Politics. Peter Allen, Oxford University Press. © Oxford University Press (2025).
DOI: 10.1093/9780197679395.003.0002

But this was power that they shouldn't have had—their possession of power was not legitimate.

If we grant these critiques the generosity of taking them at face value (and not purely as ideational posturing), we see in them an assertion that power—in this case the power to affect one's physical surroundings—should flow through institutions that exist to ensure it is used in a certain way by certain people. These institutions legitimize the exercise of power. And implicit in this assertion lies an assumption that these institutions are both fundamentally good and fundamentally neutral, treating all who seek to use them to bring about change in the same way. At corporate away days, a common team-building exercise dictates that participants are only permitted to speak when in possession of an oversized red ball which is then passed to a colleague so that they can do the same. The red ball indicates that you have the floor. In the same way, this vision of power sees it as akin to the big red ball. Only she in possession of the red ball may speak. Only they in possession of the requisite approval from the appropriate democratic body may remove the statue of the slaver. In this framing, and under these assumptions, the question of how one might come to hold the ball remains unaddressed as does the question of why the ball is so important—who decided to use this red ball system anyway?

Keir Starmer's comments suggest that he agrees with the outcome—the statue being removed—but not how it was brought about. The protesters weren't holding the ball. Had Starmer looked into the issue more deeply, he may have known that various community groups and individual citizens in Bristol had over the years sought to either remove the statue of Colston or augment it with a plaque that detailed Colston's role in the slave trade and the numbers of people who lost their lives as a result of his business practices. These attempts were, however, blocked by an "organization of rich and influential business people" who stymied efforts to bring about change through what Keir Starmer would presumably consider a process that offered "consent" for the decision.[3]

When we zoom out from the incident, we no longer see it as about who holds the ball, but about access to the ball—to the right to change society—in the first place. Zooming out highlights the fact that all are not equally able to engage with those formal processes in the same way—those who the rules of the game were shaped by and structured around are in the best position to understand and probe them for potential weaknesses. They know which buttons to press. Focusing on the question of who holds the ball strips away context from what happened, making it a question of personal morality, of unwarranted power and rule-breaking, masking the fact that this ignored context contains, preserves and grants other kinds of power. Less visible kinds, perhaps, but more permanent and embedded and harder, much harder, to argue are illegitimate.

When political events happen there is a textbook story that we are often told—one where power is clearly held by identifiable individuals and where there are formal mechanisms through which they are held to account. This is the influential story laid out by American political scientists in the 1950s and that for the most part, still underpins the way that politics is discussed today. But the reality is more complex. In reality power operates between, above, and underneath the formal channels and mechanisms that we often think of when we think about power. It is this tension between visible power and invisible power, the question of how we control these different kinds of power and, ultimately, what this means for the way our societies work that is the focus of this chapter. Power comes in different forms, some of which will not always be immediately apparent at first glance. Identifying power can be difficult work. But it is essential work all the same given that identification is a necessary precursor to the exercise of critiquing power: we cannot critique what we cannot identify.

Power is about who gets to do what, but also what it is that anybody gets to do. What, if any, are the consequences for doing certain things? Power is about enforcing the rules but also writing the rules. Power, in short, is about almost everything in politics and consequently it runs through this whole book. But we start with a discussion that I hope will allow you to see power—really see it—in all its guises. And once you do, you will see it everywhere.

Too Tight, Too Loose

You see a man in a suit at a podium. A woman applauded in Parliament. Cars with blacked-out windows and armed guards. These things look like power. We know that whoever is at the center of these situations is powerful. Usually, their power stems from constitutions or other formalized and longstanding arrangements that decide who is allowed to control the apparatus of the state and, in short, tell others what to do.

When we think of political power, we often think of this. The story goes roughly as follows: as societies, we have collectively agreed (usually over time) to give up certain freedoms to a state that in return offers us some measure of protection and support. Sometimes these arrangements are written down in a single document (a constitution) while others are more haphazard and loose, spread across numerous historical artifacts. On this account, politics is about who controls this state and the tools it offers. In some places, state control is achieved through brute force or is passed down through a bloodline. In others, more or less free and fair processes of election see different political figures and groupings compete to win popular support for their proposals of what to do with the power of the state. Obtaining power this way is legitimate, these processes acting as an authorizing stamp of sorts. These are what we call democracies, and this, I imagine, is what is familiar to most of you who are reading these words. In all of these political systems—democracies, autocracies, monarchies—this kind of traditional political power is the kind of power that you can see and, in many cases, reach out and touch. It is interesting but not mysterious. Its sources are clear.

This is part one of a two-part story about power. This part tells us that there is a single tap from which power can flow, and that flow is carefully controlled. People can only legitimately obtain power through certain means and citizens are able to identify those who have it. In electoral democracies, this sense of controlling power is fundamental to the systems we live under. Controlling who gets power in this way makes it easy to identify who has it and who doesn't. It also has the result that when those who have it through electoral means use power, we can be fairly sure they are using it legitimately—they are holding the ball.

Visibility is a double-edged sword for power and those who wield it. On the one hand, power often works precisely because others can see it (there is a reason that nightclub bouncers tend to come from the end of the height distribution labeled "gigantic"). But on the other, the obvious use of it transforms power into a target for others to aim for (ask any tall friends of yours how often someone tries to start something when they are in a busy bar on a Friday night). In countries with active opposition parties and a free press with license to be critical, it is expected—encouraged—that the powerful will loom larger in the public sphere than the average citizen and that this will help us to control the power they wield. To put it another way, they will have to answer for their actions and their choices: they cannot just do whatever they want. Not only is who gets power controlled, so is what they do with it. If we have any suspicion that power is being used in an illegitimate way, we have some recourse. This is where the second part of the story comes in—the notion of accountability.

What do we mean by accountability? To some extent, this is a question of how far we are willing to go. Some accountability is brutal—think of a guillotine or a firing squad following a coup. But among democratic forms of accountability—those premised on some notion of equality and due process—there remains great variety. Some states offer answers to a number of these questions in documents of constitution. The United States constitution, for example, outlines multiple routes to the impeachment of the president by the Congress and contains a relatively clear (though open to interpretation) list of offenses that are deemed serious enough to instigate the impeachment process. If the impeachment process is ultimately successful the president is removed from office. For around 450 years up until the nineteenth century, the UK had a similar impeachment process that was to be used to prosecute members of the government who stood accused of "high crimes and misdemeanors, beyond the reach of the law or which no other authority in the state will prosecute."[4] Now, it is expected that parliamentary accountability combined with legal recourse via judicial review will serve this purpose. If this sounds a bit dry, that's kind of the point. Being detached and impersonal is a feature, not a bug.

Formal accountability pursued within a democratic political system exists, then, but nowadays predominantly has a flavor of scrutiny, where the aim of the accountability process is to uncover, to probe, and to expose. There is some room to punish offenders, but even at the extreme this is generally limited to removing them from the political office they hold. This is no small thing, but unless combined with the ingredients of legal culpability, the recourse is largely political, not personal. A curtailed political career ending in some variety of public disgrace is bad, no doubt, but it is neither imprisonment nor impoverishment. Overall, it arguably makes sense to separate political and criminal wrongdoing in order to prevent bad actors from pursuing their political enemies via criminal procedures. But we have to retain an awareness that the choice to bracket one form of misconduct as criminal and another as (merely) political is that—a choice. Taking the UK as an example, it may well be true that standard criminal law is a bad fit for diagnosing, prosecuting, and punishing the misdemeanors of politicians. But even bad fits—things that are too tight in one place and too loose in another and sometimes both at the same time—can be adjusted to fit better. Many of the things I am thinking about here—misleading the public or ignoring key pieces of evidence in decision-making about policies—*are* a bad fit for criminal proceedings, but the formal process of pursuing some sort of justice via mechanisms of political accountability equally feels too baggy. And "baggy" is the word, as they give the wearer, our leaders, significant freedom to wriggle. Power can be used in the knowledge that once in motion, it might never again be constrained.

If someone were to approach somebody else in the street and beat them to death—undeniably a show of power—this would not be a legitimate display of power. We have codified the illegitimacy of this act in law, and the person can be prosecuted and punished for having committed a crime. But most cases in politics are less clear. If a war is started by a lie, and many die as a result, did the propagator of the lie kill them in some way? If funding is removed from a lifesaving service and lives are no longer saved, is the person counting the money a killer? Or, because the people doing these things do them from the vantage point of an elected political office, is our ability to potentially remove them from that office sufficient accountability for what they do while in them? If politicians willingly take on more power than the average citizen—more power than the rest of us—maybe the standards they are held to, and the scope of things those standards cover, should be higher and broader than for everyone else? Where should we draw the line?

Seeing What We Want To

Accountability as described above is not solely about the enforcement of rules but also the rules themselves. What standard will we use to judge the actions of those in power? Formal political accountability has a selective gaze. Constitutions, either written or assembled, are not omniscient. They only look for certain kinds of wrongdoing, their capacity for detection is limited by design.

There is wrongdoing that they do not want to see and only certain behaviors or actions can be counted when a reckoning takes place. It is not simply a question of how effectively the rules are kept to in any given case, but whether or not a specific case is even considered to be worthy of enforcement in the first place and whether the kinds of enforcement we might expect or desire are on the table at all. Power has a role at both stages.[5] Power and influence can be used by those who have it to define away certain activities or behaviors as outside the scope of accountability—the formal version of turning a blind eye. Power shapes the rules. And if the powerful and influential nonetheless do fall prey to the rules in some way, they have the power, influence, and attendant resources to better work within the system that—don't forget—they would likely have had some role in assembling in the first place. Imagine a game where the referee and writer of the rules of the sport also happens to be the best player on the pitch and you'll begin to get the idea. The issue here is that in order to work, accountability needs some authority behind it. If those same sources of authority are likely to benefit from a generalized lack of accountability, they are unlikely to support it in specific cases or spheres.

If politicians tell us they are going to pursue some policy that we can have some certainty will cause a nontrivial amount of suffering for some section of the population, does the fact that they have told us this, admitted it, exempt them from additional (nonelectoral) accountability regarding the consequences of that policy? Is it the case that their telling us this makes this a political question—that is, whether those people should suffer as a result of that policy becomes a political judgment to be made through the established democratic mechanisms. These political questions thereby become somehow distinct from the simpler, cleaner issue of an MP being jailed for expenses fraud, despite it being obvious that the latter is relatively trivial in terms of its consequences by comparison to the former. Of course, this might be the point—it is easier to grab the low-hanging fruit of easy morality tales ("she stole from the taxpayer") than the complicated and slippery bounty that reflect more systematic patterns of wrongdoing ("he instigated economic policies that led to changes in the welfare system that subsequently have driven thousands to immiseration and death over the course of a decade"). What interests me here is what would cause us to shift something back, to make something not a legitimate political question anymore. For there must be a line somewhere. It seems perverse to accept (or, worse, to insist) that proposing policies that will immiserate vast swathes of the citizenry is just business as usual, legitimate politics.

The past two decades have seen British politicians make many decisions that appear to have been based on spurious or misleading grounds, that have caused significant material loss to ordinary citizens, or that have risked lives through either negligence or incompetence. Despite this, there is a pervasive sense that nothing happens or changes as a result—either for the individuals in question or for the broader structures of society. Take George Osborne, for example, the former finance minister (known as the chancellor of the exchequer) of the UK from 2010 to 2017. Osborne oversaw a widespread program of austerity, which is broadly speaking the reduction of state spending. The withdrawal of state services and the lowering of financial support provided by the state is estimated to have had a role in the deaths of 100,000 citizens.[6] This is more than the number of home front deaths during the second world war. This number also fails to take into account the impact of Osborne's austerity program on the National Health Service, specifically its ability to respond to the outbreak of the COVID-19 pandemic in early 2020. As I write, this pandemic has resulted in the deaths of at least a further 230,000 Britons.[7]

Osborne, and the prime minister he worked under, David Cameron, justified the austerity program on the basis that the United Kingdom would "go bust" if it did not reduce its deficit as lenders would have no confidence that the country could service future debt obligations. This was not an accurate depiction of the situation. Instead, Osborne's move to implement austerity should be seen as a political choice, not an inevitable necessity. It was a political choice to make the decision to cut state spending, a choice to cut it in the specific areas in which the cuts mainly fell, and a choice to persevere with the strategy in the face of mounting evidence and testimony of its effects. It seems unlikely that Osborne did these things, bringing about these adverse effects, in ignorance. For example, the Institute for Fiscal Studies warned in 2011 that the austerity agenda that the government was pursuing would render it "inconceivable that [the] Government will get close to its 2020 child poverty targets under current policies" and that lower income households, especially families with children, would be hit hardest by austerity.[8] Acknowledging and recognizing this helps us to refine our question above. What we would need to judge is whether these kinds of political choices, made while in positions of power, leave the decision-maker culpable for their effects and, if they do, why is this the case? This is a different kind of question about legitimacy—is the legitimacy of the use of power not just about the source of that power, but also about the substance of what that power was used for?

If there is a broad agreement among those with power and influence and resources that some things should never be brought into the frame when it comes to accountability measures—that is, generally by avoiding having accountability measures that affect politicians in an individual or personal way—then, simply, they won't. I am not necessarily saying that they *should*, but the point is that the formal rules here are underpinned by the interests of those who already hold that power and influence, not by those who don't and who therefore may be less sanguine about people judged to have done wrong losing it.

Much of the time, we can see who wrote the rules. We can identify the individuals and organizations involved in their drafting, their adoption, and their implementation. And in a roundabout way, there are usually processes for removing these people for certain kinds of wrongdoing—for breaking other sets of rules.

Sometimes this is removing them via elections (voting them out), but other times it might take the form of judicial or legal intervention. Either way, their power can be curtailed, not least because the power they have is the kind we can see—it is codified in rules, laws, statutes, documents, and so on. To some extent, you can reach out and touch it.

The complicating factor here is that the rules we can see being written (by people we can remove from office, theoretically) are underpinned and upheld by a series of other rules that we can't see and that we can't vote out. These exist in the practices, norms, and daily life of the institutions that surround us—they went in with the bricks. We can think of this as something like structural power, a form of power that we have an unequal ability to deploy in the pursuit of our ends—when we choose to act, we do so from a certain position among social relations that give us more or less power to control how our lives go.

Dark Matter

Cosmologists believe that dark matter exists because they can see its effects on other things. It is present by insinuation: it is the disturbed papers on the desk of a murder victim, the smudged fingerprint on a shard of weaponized glass, the vague hint of a distinctive perfume hanging around the body. And the kind of power I am talking about—power that operates largely in the background of societies, unelected and not invested in specific roles of given offices—similarly shows itself to us in outline through its interactions with other things, perhaps most clearly those mechanisms that we as a society use to hold formal power to account, like the press and the criminal justice system, but also in interactions with institutions of all kinds.

Structures, and structural power, are not alien to everyday thinking. When we discuss professional sports, for example, we regularly discuss big clubs and small clubs. We acknowledge that some clubs are likely to perform better over a season because they are better resourced. This gives them opportunities to get a head start on their opponents in the form of improved training facilities, more comfortable travel arrangements and, of course, buying the most talented players. It is hard to imagine that football fans and pundits would insist on day one of the new season that they felt each team had an equal opportunity to win the league and, if they didn't, this must be down to some failing on the team's part. The dark matter of soccer is money—if we asked someone to analyze the reason that Manchester City have won four out of the last five Premier League titles without reference to their 2008 takeover by Emerati billionaire, Sheikh Mansour, we would not expect to learn much from the exercise. We accept that there are circumstances and conditions that exist outside of the control of any individual player (or indeed any given team) that leave some better placed to do this than others. The dark matter explains why things are the way they are in a grand sense.

Similarly, why would we expect any serious analysis of the societies we live in to occur without taking account of the following kinds of statistics? Of all housing wealth in the UK, 46 percent is held by those born before 1950.[9] Thirty percent of children in the UK live in poverty.[10] The average income of the top 0.01 percent of American households increased nine times more quickly between 1979 and 2019 than the income of the bottom 20 percent.[11] July 20, 2020 saw then CEO of Amazon, Jeff Bezos, increase his wealth by $10 billion in a single day.[12] In 2018–2019, "42 percent of all disposable household income in the UK went to the 20 percent of people with the highest household incomes, while 7 percent went to the lowest-income 20 percent."[13] Data from 2023 from the US Bureau of Labor Statistics suggests that among American workers, the median white worker is likely to earn 25 percent more than the median Black worker and 28 percent more than the median Latino worker.[14] Ethnic minority households in the UK are the most likely to live in persistent poverty.[15] A 2017 government report on racial disparity in the UK found that "around 1 in 10 adults from a Black, Pakistani, Bangladeshi or Mixed background were unemployed compared with 1 in 25 White British people."[16] Black Americans, on average, have a life expectancy over three years lower than white Americans.[17]

This dark matter structures everything around it even if we cannot see it directly. It often becomes visible, so to speak, when some series of events combine to show what the previously unspoken default settings of a given situation are assumed to be. These inequalities are, in different ways, also inequalities of power. They are inequalities of power to access certain opportunities, inequalities in the security and assurance of definitely having somewhere to live, and inequality in how you are rewarded for the work you do. Such inequality means that any new government policy, any change in how the world works, essentially anything happening, will affect people differently depending on where they sit in relation to these kinds of inequality. Owning your home will mean that rental increases are not your problem. Having some savings in the bank means that a domestic appliance malfunctioning will not leave you hungry for the rest of the month. In general, though not always, living at the sharp end of these inequalities will render you relatively less powerful compared to those who do not, something that feels increasingly true as the brute force of wealth allows those who possess lots of it to live more and more sequestered lives.

Society is shaped in such a way that makes a series of assumptions about who will do what. There are default settings programmed into all we see around us. For example, it is assumed that certain jobs are for certain kinds of people, certain housing the same. Certain spaces are welcoming to some and hostile to others. This probably sounds familiar to you. These assumptions reflect power and to understand power better, we should question who fits with these assumptions—who benefits from them?—and who does not.

A Sense of Comfort

When they are working in your favor, what is it that these assumptions can give you? A comfort? A sense that regardless of how events proceed, you will be okay somehow? This comfort gives you greater freedom to act, and a greater sense that you can make things happen that you want to. You have probably experienced something like this, moving from a situation or environment where you felt comfortable and assured to another where you feel the opposite. Our feelings of comfort or discomfort are often rooted in the kind of upbringing we had, most notably our social class. The sociologist Pierre Bourdieu identified this phenomenon, referring to it as your *habitus*—a sort of programming that guides you as you move through the world that is rooted in social class.[18] You might have had the experience of walking into a Michelin-starred fine dining restaurant and immediately feeling like you do not belong or had the same feeling when walking into a small neighborhood bar. In both cases, your sense of yourself and the situations in which you found yourself did not match.

In Sally Rooney's coming-of-age novel *Normal People* readers see the eighteen-year-old protagonists and on-off couple, Marianne and Connell, make the transition from high school to university. At school, working-class Connell is popular, comfortable in his surroundings. He knows how the social system of school functions, how to do the right thing. Middle-class Marianne, conversely, is outcast at school, largely friendless, lacking the kind of currency that is required to succeed socially. When the pair move on to university at Trinity College Dublin, these social capacities are reversed. Marianne, it transpires, possesses the capital that permits social status at Trinity, while Connell, in spite of his clear intellectual abilities, does not. This capital, as it turns out, is the original kind—wealth. The dynamics of power in the relationship between Marianne and Connell shift during this time, with Connell's previous upper hand in this regard now gone (at college he largely hangs out with her friends, not she with his).[19] Connell notices that "his classmates are not like him . . . They just move through the world in a different way, and he'll probably never really understand them, and he knows they will never understand him, or even try."[20] Power, we (and Connell) see, is contextual. What grants power, what counts as useful in its pursuit, changes depending on the situation. To put this in Bourdieuian terms, Marianne and Connell possess different forms of habitus. These endow them with different kinds of capital that can be applied to generate differential returns across different fields.

The revelation that underpinned Bourdieu's analysis was that social class affected much more than the amount of money—capital—in your bank account or on your asset sheet. Social class was not just about what one has, but who one is. We are by now familiar with terms such as "cultural capital" and "social capital," but perhaps fail to see them in our daily lives, while we are at work, socializing, or simply existing in public.[21] In their book *The Class Ceiling: Why It Pays to Be Privileged*, sociologists Sam Friedman and Daniel Laurison explore the role of social class in the workplaces of elite occupations including a television channel, architecture practice, accountancy firm. Interviewing staff at different levels of seniority at these places sees many of them speak about unwritten rules, informal norms, "the way things are done around here." When the rules aren't written down, at least not all of them and often the ones that make the most difference, it is up to individuals to try and figure them out on their own. In one sense, this could serve as a sort of test, where prospective colleagues have to navigate these unwritten social and practical mores from a standing start and whoever does best gets the job or promotion. But the nature of these rules is such that they have formed in a way that leaves some of those trying to navigate them at a standing start and puts others ten meters ahead from the very beginning. How so? Because the unwritten rules were largely constructed by, and for, a certain kind of person and, historically, the people in power at elite workplaces were white, middle- and upper-class men. To think like Bourdieu once again, the rules are constructed around certain kinds of embodied cultural and social capital that are more likely to exist in some bodies than in others, generally along the lines of class, race, and gender. Assuming that the rules are neutral, insensitive to any variation or difference among those seeking to figure them out, is foolish.

Zadie Smith's novel *NW* follows two young girls growing up in northwest London as they navigate issues of class, race, and sex. At one point, Natalie, a Black woman and one of the protagonists who the reader follows from her working-class upbringing to her against-the-odds success in the legal profession, gets advice from a senior colleague, also a Black woman, named Theodora:

> When I first started appearing before a judge, I kept being reprimanded from the bench. I was losing my cases and I couldn't understand why. Then I realized the following: when some floppy-haired chap from Surrey stands before these judges, all his passionate arguments read as "pure advocacy." He and the judge recognize each other. They are understood by each other. Very likely went to the same school. But Whaley's passion, or mine, or yours, reads as "aggression." To the judge. This is his house and you are an interloper within it. And let me tell you, with a woman it's worse: "aggressive hysteria." The first lesson is: turn yourself down. One notch. Two. Because this is not neutral.[22]

Friedman and Laurison discuss this process of fitting in as akin to a glass slipper: as with Cinderella, for some people the shoe just fits, with little effort required on their part. Each elite occupation has its own glass slipper, a way of being that is accepted as the "best" way to be in that place, a way of being that, if one can achieve it, marks you out as the kind of person who will be good at that job. But as Natalie discovers in *NW*, some approach this challenge at an advantage. Friedman and Laurison, again:

The particular "glass slippers" for different occupations, then, are about their histories, about what type of people tended to do this kind of work in the past and how their ideas about the "right" way to act at work have become embedded, even institutionalised, over time.[23]

This idea of intangible factors facilitating a sense of personal, social, and professional ease will, I expect, be familiar to many British readers. I grew up in southeast greater London and, purely as a product of this chance event that was (and remains) totally outside of my control, I speak with what is known as an Estuary accent. "Estuary" has variously been described as "classless" and as an accent whose "level of prestige is increasing" (this fact is unrelated to my possession of the accent).[24] For better or worse, Tony Blair is perhaps one of the most famous speakers with the accent and is additionally exemplary of the ability of the accent to scale the class ladder as needed. For example, the accent can slide down the ladder to "Cockney" or climb up to "R.P." (Received Pronunciation), depending on the context. I certainly feel I have benefitted from the way this fluke of geography has caused me to speak, with acquaintances telling me I sound "relaxing," "authoritative," and "posh." Crucially, my actual upbringing (my habitus) was, for want of a better word, normal (my parents worked in the public sector and I attended state schools). As such, while I am in no position to comment on whether any of these things said about my accent are true, I suspect what my admirers are actually getting at is that I sound a bit like most of the voices they hear from sources considered as relaxing (audiobooks, for example), authoritative (BBC Radio), and posh (some TV dramas). Estuary is beneficial because it puts the listener in mind of things that carry cultural kudos. It gives the speaker—me, in this case—a head start, an ability to choose the direction of travel, in social terms, of my own voice and, in turn, exert some control over how I may be perceived. David Rosewarne, who first coined the term "Estuary English," noted of the accent that "for many British people [it] is beginning to take over one of the traditional functions of R.P., that of disguising origins."[25] The ongoing necessity of such a cover-up was confirmed by one of Friedman and Laurison's interviewees at a large accountancy firm, who said "When I hear people using incorrect grammar or things like that, it's a very obvious identifier of something, a regional dialect that hasn't been tempered."[26]

Ultimately, then, what this adds up to is the legitimation of certain ways of being, of thinking about things, and of consuming things as somehow superior to others. Context-dependent, this will leave some people at an advantage relative to others. As a consequence of the historical marginalization of women, the working class, and people of color (among other marginalized groups) from institutions and sites of social power over time, these places overwhelmingly legitimate the dominant (white, male, middle and upper class) group's dispositions and patterns of behavior while downgrading those seen as different, as impinging on "the norm." Those who study the world of competitive sport have now established as fact the idea of home-field advantage—the phenomenon by which teams playing in their home stadium or venue tend to produce better outcomes (usually measured by more wins or achieving a higher score) than when playing away from home.[27] There are multiple potential explanations for this—having more of your fans cheering you on, familiarity with the environment both before and during the game, being able to sleep in your own home the night before the game and avoid a long trip to travel to the stadium, and so on. The kind of structural power I am talking about is similar to home-field advantage. It doesn't guarantee a winning result, but it makes it more likely. If you lose anyway, it limits the damage. The environment and infrastructure around you is familiar to you, comfortable even. You are playing, to put it another way, at home.

At the individual level, what does this grant those who can, somehow, fit in? I think it is best characterized as an ease of movement, a flow. Of being noticed when you want to be and invisible when you don't. Of being listened to, being seen. Of being taken seriously, being counted. Over time, both as individuals and as a society, it becomes more and more apparent who is seen to belong in some spaces and not in others. Who counts in some places and not in others, and who is conspicuous in some places and not in others. Who gets to exist and who gets to flourish. Who gets to speak and who doesn't. A more prosaic example of this works through taste, specifically taste in consumer items. In the final volume of his *My Struggle* series of books, Karl Ove Knausgaard discusses these ideas in the context of purchasing various goods:

> The whole of this enormous world, teeming with detail, was divided into intricate, finely meshed systems that kept every-thing apart . . . infusing the various goods or services with value, thereby grading them in ways no school could ever teach, and which therefore had to be learned ad hoc, outside any school or institution, and which furthermore were forever in a state of flux . . . This knowledge was not written down anywhere, and it was hardly accepted as knowledge at all, it was more an assur-ance regarding the way things stood, and it fluctuated according to the social strata in such a way that someone from the upper classes would be able to frown on my sofa preferences and the sofa knowledge I was thereby demonstrating, just as I in turn would be able to frown on the taste in sofas of people belonging to a lower status group than myself.[28]

Familiarity with this kind of knowledge too is power. It is dif-ferent to the power of a prime minister or president, but it is power nonetheless. It is also a kind of power that is hard to account for in the traditional ways we discuss power, in terms of legitimacy, illegitimacy, or accountability. We have no formalized system for determining who gets this power. We have no process for holding it accountable for its use. And, for some, it is a kind of power that does not exist, rather it is something that people—the so-called woke—have dreamed up in order to fill the gap left by the apparently now-resolved issues of racism, sexism, and homophobia.[29] As Douglas Murray, the right-wing political commentator, writes:

> It was inevitable that some pitch would be made for the deserted ground . . . The question of what exactly we are meant to do now—other than get rich where we can and have whatever fun is on offer—was going to have to be answered by something. The answer that has presented itself in recent years is to engage in new battles, ever fiercer campaigns and ever more niche demands. To find meaning by waging a constant war against anybody who seems to be on the wrong side of a question which may itself have just been reframed and the answer to which has only just been altered.[30]

But refusing to countenance the possibility that structures and institutions and resources can transmit and bestow power to some and not to others is difficult. Is it really plausible to account for—justify—the kinds of inequalities listed earlier without needing something unseen, some dark matter, to do quite a lot of heavy lifting? It isn't, and many refuseniks on the issue of structural imbalances of power adopt ideas of meritocracy and the associated notions of effort, aspiration, and hard work to fill the gap in their theory. But why would we assume effort, aspiration, and hard work to map closely onto characteristics like race, gender, age, geographic location, or social class? Up until a few years ago, I would here write that a defense of this idea was largely inconceivable in mainstream discourse but, sadly, that is no longer the case. Many who are unwilling to acknowledge even the possible existence of structural relations of power within society are now happy—even lauded—for saying precisely these things (Murray, who I quote above, is increasingly present as a pundit and writer on both sides of the Atlantic). The dark matter remains in the dark.

Power can benefit from a lack of visibility—the material benefits of power remain untouched, but it exists unacknowledged. The
dark matter becomes even harder to detect, harder to account for.
In a 2005 commencement speech at Kenyon College, the late writer
David Foster Wallace deployed a "didactic little parable-ish" (his
words) story as part of his address:

> There are these two young fish swimming along and they happen
> to meet an older fish swimming the other way, who nods at them
> and says "Morning, boys. How's the water?" And the two young
> fish swim on for a bit, and then eventually one of them looks over
> at the other and goes "What the hell is water?"[31]

When we refuse to acknowledge that power will not always
show up in a suit, surrounded by the Secret Service, are we
any better than these young fish? "Morning, boys. How are the
structural power relations in society?" Confused faces. "What
the hell is power?" Wallace calls on the graduating students to
"bracket . . . your skepticism about the value of the totally obvious." Without a fuller appreciation of power, we will continue to
be baffled by things that ultimately are not that baffling at all.

Why Would You Throw a Statue Into a River?

Let's think again about statues, power, and home-fields. Do those
responses referring to mobs and authoritarian control stand up to
scrutiny? Arguably, the "mob" in the case of Colston is not drawing
on pre-existing power sources in society; it is a largely spontaneous
grouping, in this case of somewhat disenfranchised individuals,
who gain whatever power they have from that connectedness. The
protest here is a temporary grab for power, a move for autonomy,
an attempt to create an environment in which the structural power
imbalances they normally face no longer hold them back. If we ask

the question of who really has the crowd on their side, the answer is clearly those who are able to activate and rely on the broader structures of power in society from which they draw their authority and sustenance. The protesters, once dispersed, lack any of this power until, or if, they once again come together. In terms of who actually has any realistic prospect of controlling the conditions under which we as a society live, if this is obviously true of the Home Secretary, the Leader of the Opposition (now the prime minister), and influential academics, it is most certainly not true of the protesters, not a single one of whom I, or anyone else, could spontaneously name. The political scientist, Colin Hay, tells us that power is "about context-shaping, about the capacity of actors to redefine the parameters of what is socially, politically and economically possible for others."[32] If the protesters held power in terms of their immediate actions, it seems clear that when it comes to shaping the wider legal, social, and economic context, they do not. In other words, they lack the power to influence what other people want in terms of political or social outcomes. Think again about who *does* have the power to do that in our society.

The reaction to these events is also often an exercise in self-exculpation, in avoiding the tricky but pressing question of why it seems to be the case that a group of citizens felt that the only way to achieve a nonviolent political change, one that would not result in personal enrichment, was to work outside of the established system? Rather than rush to condemn these actions as criminal, there is surely some benefit to be found in exploring their motivation. It is by now cliché to highlight the fact that many of the major events and developments that politicians, and citizens in democracies, point to as evidence of societal progress were brought about in this way. By working outside of existing political structures, almost all of which claimed to be democratic but now would not be considered so in the slightest, the civil rights movement in the United States ended Jim Crow segregation laws, the Suffragettes won the vote for British women, and Nelson Mandela and the ANC resisted and eventually overcame apartheid in South Africa. Democracies have long witnessed these patterns, whereby citizens push and pull at established norms, probing the rules to achieve what history eventually comes to see as more democratic outcomes. Democracy, in this view, is not a bottomless well of respect and obedience to a static set of institutions or rules that exist outside of a given context. Instead, democracy is perhaps better characterized as consisting in political equality and the pursuit of this ideal. And sometimes that pursuit will take place outside of whatever the dominant notions of democracy are in a society at any given moment. Why would you throw a statue into a river? Maybe because you realized that the game was rigged. And if something is rigged, blatantly so, why bother playing by the rules?

As consumers of news coverage of events such as this one, we need to do our best to think about them in terms of power. In this case, it would be very simple, even comforting, to accept the dominant framing of the mob running riot, breaking the law, damaging property, and so on. And if the protest had been violent against others not involved, or been an indiscriminate rampage that put bystanders in danger, this may have been more justified. But those things did not happen. Instead, this dominant framing removes any actual political content from the actions of those involved and in doing so, both obscures and reproduces the very imbalances in power that produced the protests in the first place. As citizens, we owe it to one another to look twice, look harder.

Getting Away with It

The fundamental difficulty from which many of the issues I have discussed stem can be stated simply: a small number of individuals enter public life in an effort to exert control over things that affect the private lives of others, often without their own private lives being put on the table. By private life, I don't mean their sexual habits or the schooling choices they make for their children, but the broader course of their lives—how well their lives go, in the grand scheme of things. This distinction is hardened by social inequality as certain groups of citizens disproportionately suffer for a disproportionate amount of time in cycles of poverty and deprivation, while others, conversely, prosper and hold formal political power on what feels like a more or less permanent basis.[33]

Osborne's austerity program changed the lives of many Britons for the worse. Sarah-Marie Hall, an academic geographer, has undertaken countless interviews with individuals and families affected by austerity policies, including people whose benefit payments from the state were cut, lost employment as a result of broader economic contraction, or who found themselves in precarious housing situations. One of her interviewees, a woman called Selma, who lived with her daughter in social housing and survived on welfare payments from the government, told Hall that "life is hard . . . I have no money, it's very very hard."[34] Hall reflected on the time she spent with Selma during the course of her research:

> Throughout her eight months taking part in the research, I observed these struggles for Selma up close; at supermarket tills counting out the last of her coins, at home measuring out small batches of minced lamb for the freezer so they could eat that week, or getting three buses instead of one because her weekly pass enabled travel with only one operator. The accumulation of these personal strains took their toll on Selma and other participants, often describing themselves as tired—physically, mentally, and of their precarious situation.

Even reading about this accrual of subtle indignities and inconveniences is exhausting. The overwhelming majority of people do not hold the kind of power that allows them to reshape the rules in a way more favorable to themselves, nor do they possess the social, financial, and cultural resources that would allow them to navigate the rules in a seamless and advantageous way when they come into conflict with them. When those with power are seen to do both—shape and navigate—there comes a general feeling that they are getting away with something. There is a sense that above and beyond accountability, there should be some genuine punishment or redress. It isn't enough to be exposed—something has to happen to the offender.

Osborne was held to account for his decisions as far as the formal methods of political accountability in the UK would allow—parliamentary scrutiny, media inquiry, and so on—and he did ultimately lose his position as Chancellor following the Brexit referendum in 2016. But in many other ways, he has lost nothing. Materially, at least, Osborne is in a stronger position than ever. Happily for him, it turns out that what waits at the intersection of a failed political career and the possession of enormous capital of all kinds is a well-paid and influential newspaper editorship, a spot in the co-host's chair on a popular podcast, advisory roles in investment banks, and the chairmanship of the British Museum—positions of significant influence over the cultural and political life of the UK. So whatever mechanisms of accountability he has faced don't seem to have affected him beyond a relatively narrow scope—he has retained, and gained, power that exists beyond the grasp of formal consequences.

But societies are not only, not even mainly, about formal consequences. Living in a society is about living within a series of informal frameworks that guide and shape expectations of behavior. Often these expectations are positive, looking to induce behaviors that the society wants—this is why those who raise large amounts of money for charity are publicly praised, for example. Perhaps equally often, though, these norms are about sanctioning behaviors that are not desirable, behaviors that we want less of. And a great deal of sanctioning takes the form of shaming those who have not conformed to the norms being imposed in order to "hold individuals to the group standard."[35] Jennifer Jacquet, a psychologist, writes that "exposure is the essence of shaming, and a feeling of exposure is also one of shame's (the emotion) most distinct ingredients and intimately links shame to reputation."[36] Jacquet, though, is keen to highlight the distinction between *shaming*, which is the regulation of behavior through exposure in front of an audience, to the feeling of shame, which instead is self-regulatory, a feeling that is perceived within an individual and causes them to adjust their behavior accordingly (or doesn't in some cases—Jacquet describes how many serial killers, for example, appear to be unable to feel what most of us mean when we say we feel shame for some behavior of ours).

Processes of formal political accountability, and associated media coverage, are about shaming in a broad sense—exposing somebody's actions and speculating about the motivation behind them. But in an unspoken and informal way, democratic societies have also traditionally relied on the notion of shame (as self-regulation) as a method of accountability. Shame, and the anticipation of what might happen as a result of undertaking some action, has controlled the behavior of those with power. Much of this comes as a result of the internalization of norms, the ways that things are done in a given context. We have seen many examples of this in politics, not least surrounding various processes that take place in political institutions. For example, politicians will not sit in certain places, or associate with certain people, for fear of the imagined feelings of shame that might result from these actions being visible.

But right now, we have a surplus of shaming and a surfeit of shame. And for most who hold political power, a further surfeit of material consequences. Our formal mechanisms are generally not designed for this (barring obviously criminal cases), so the punishment must happen informally, socially, through norms—but the vehicles through which this happens (vehicles of social influence like the media) do not either focus on, or affect, all offenders equally (and will often selectively pick which offenders/offenses to focus on). Punishment is not uniformly felt.

Does Osborne *feel* shame for his decisions and their effects? Or is he, in regard to his decisions during his political career at least, shameless? I would argue that if we as citizens are resorting to hoping that our politicians feel shame for decisions that have nonetheless been effectively validated by the various arms of our political system that are meant to provide accountability, permit redress, and avoid wrongdoing, have we not already lost? Would we feel better if a denuded Osborne was forced to live under the benefits regime he created? Maybe. Fundamentally, shamelessness is rooted in a sense that one is outside of—above—the indignities of the daily lives of everybody else. It is an amplification of the sense that we all have that we are the star of our own show. Perhaps the difference is that the truly shameless believe they are not just the star of their show, but of all shows. The issue for representative democracy is that queasy as this assertion may make us, what it describes is not that far off the reality of our situation.[37] There does appear to exist a class of person in liberal democracies who is able to exist outside of the quotidian that most others navigate. This elevation beyond the normal is in no way mysterious: it comes from wealth, privilege, an abundance of resources concentrated in the hands of the few. It is a problem when, as a result, leaders and the led do not share in the same fate, a fate controlled overwhelmingly by the former and experienced most intensely, and uncomfortably, by the latter.

2

Think About Knowledge

Talking Shit

In early 2017 the former England soccer player Gary Lineker, now a presenter of sports coverage on television, made a series of statements in opposition to various newly proposed policies restricting the movement of refugees from war zones primarily in Syria. Around the same time, the author of the *Harry Potter* series, J. K. Rowling, expressed her opposition to the policies of the newly inaugurated US President Donald Trump. Some users of social media platform Twitter (now X) responded with hostility:

> You were a good footballer stick to what you know about because you're talking shit about politics.[1]
> You're a grown ass woman whose entire career is based on stories about a nerd who turns people into frogs. Stay out of politics.[2]

These sorts of responses do not necessarily question the form or content of any political intervention—they don't explicitly say that they disagree with either celebrity—but rather express a kind of incredulity that the speaker has intervened at all. Instead, they are policing the boundary: the criticisms are underpinned by an assertion that these individuals simply shouldn't have gotten involved; a conviction that these individuals are in some way not qualified to do so. They do not know enough about politics to do so and are therefore not worth listening to.

The dominant story about political knowledge is that like these celebrities, most of us don't have it. A YouGov poll of UK citizens from January 2019—mere weeks before the country was set

How to Think about Politics. Peter Allen, Oxford University Press. © Oxford University Press (2025). DOI: 10.1093/9780197679395.003.0003

to leave the European Union (EU) following the saturation of news programming with terms like "Article 50," "customs union," and "backstop"—found that only half of citizens knew what the first two terms were and that even fewer understood the final term despite this being arguably the most contentious aspect of the UK's extraction from the EU.[3] Not only this, the dominant story is also that we don't even want it: given the opportunity to change, people wouldn't become more involved or engaged in politics.[4] The evidence on both of these points seems clear.

Nonetheless, this account stretches credulity in other ways. As we move through our lives we constantly deal with the state, tax authorities, and local politicians. Despite disagreeing with one another on fundamental issues, we manage to rub along with our neighbors, colleagues, and friends. We develop some sense of how we think things should go for ourselves and for other people. Is this not indicative of some kind of knowledge we might call "political"? Maybe the reality is not that people don't know that much about politics, but rather that political scientists and politicians have been looking for political knowledge in the wrong way and in the wrong places. Maybe it is time to think again.

What Kinds of Things Can We Know?

Let's start with the question of what it means to know anything at all. The branch of philosophy concerned with knowledge is known as epistemology. Those who study this area are known as epistemologists. They deal with all things epistemic. To give some examples, epistemic prowess, therefore, would refer to someone's abilities as regards what they know. Epistemic deficiency would be the opposite (what they don't know) and epistemic grounding would be the basis of something in knowledge. We might think of the epistemic grounding of climate change research as being in scientific models and data, for example. Conversely, the epistemic grounding of my knowledge about scotch whisky is hours of devoted imbibing. You get the idea.

From the moment of our arrival, life is a steady accumulation of knowledge of various kinds. We learn how to crawl, then toddle, then walk. We learn to speak, to read, to write. Some of us learn how to kick a football or swim a length, while others learn how to play the piano or strum the guitar. We learn how to make a cup of tea, boil an egg, and how to use various household appliances. These acts are easy enough to identify as knowledge—there is a skill fitting the definition of what it is we can be shown to be either able or unable to do. You either can or cannot ride a bike, for example, and your possession or otherwise of the requisite knowledge will be clear to any observer. Epistemologists refer to this kind of knowledge as knowledge-how (perhaps more familiar in the abbreviated "know-how").

A whole other way that we can be said to know something, though, is by knowing something is the case. We know that Earth is located in the Milky Way, for example, or that 2+2=4. We know that Washington, DC is the capital city of the US and that dogs have four legs. These things are propositional knowledge: "what is asserted by a sentence which says that something is the case."[5] We can think of this as knowledge-that—in contrast to knowing how to do something, we know that something is the case. Knowledge-that is perhaps most clearly demonstrated through tests of factual recall, like quizzes or exams, or simply by answering questions regarding some state of affairs.

There is extensive philosophical debate about the relationship between the two, with some arguing that knowledge-how is simply a subset of knowledge-that (i.e., that knowing how to swim is having knowledge of a series of propositions about swimming) while others have argued that know-how is an ability whereby knowledge is demonstrated practically.[6] No doubt this is an interesting sidebar (and one that does make me wonder what it means to say that I know how to swim), but it is one that I do not want to pursue too far. For the purposes of what I want to discuss in this chapter, I merely ask that you bear this distinction—of knowing how and knowing that—in mind throughout what follows.

The Magnifying Glass

The dominant narrative—that most people do not have especially high levels of political knowledge—is backed up by a sizable body of academic evidence. As the political philosopher Jason Brennan summarizes, "When it comes to politics, some people know a lot, most people know nothing, and many people know *less* than nothing."[7] Ilya Somin concurs, saying that "The reality that most voters are often ignorant of even very basic political information is one of the better-established findings of social science."[8]

Delli Carpini and Keeter found in 1993 that less than half of Americans were able to name the political party with the most seats in the US House of Representatives and less than a quarter able to name a candidate (and the candidate's party) for that same institution.[9] Fast-forward to 2010 and survey data shows low levels of knowledge among Americans regarding the state of the economy, political control of the legislative branch, and who key political figures were and what roles they held.[10] There is much other evidence that serves to confirm this, but I think you probably get the point. On the face of it, the outlook is not good—people seem to lack knowledge of politics. I am not going to try and argue otherwise; the evidence is clear. What I am going to do, though, is make a case that the existing evidence might be looking in the wrong place, missing the wood for the trees.

An occupational hazard of using social media is encountering know-it-alls. At times one is brought to wonder whether, as opposed to just being common among users, being a know-it-all is in fact a requirement of membership. Much to the detriment of my attention span (and levels of irritation), I have been a user of one social media platform, Twitter (now X), for over a decade. A benefit of this tenure is my ability to spot know-it-alls in the wild, as it were, to develop a taxonomy of traits that, when encountered, are best responded to with a quick exit from the virtual conversation. One such flag is variants of the moniker "politics geek" or "politics nerd" appearing in the small text box that Twitter allows users to fill with biographical information at the top of their profile. More than being simply a reliable signal that some boredom is headed my way, I think there is reason to be troubled by the notion of there being "politics geeks" in a deeper way.

"Politics geek" social media is the product of, and also produces, an online ecosystem that is closely wedded to the dominant and traditional figures and institutions of political life—mainstream political journalists and columnists, politicians themselves, and other individuals who work in or around politics. Our nerds and geeks swim daily in these political waters, watching rolling news, listening to political podcasts, and reading political memoirs (somebody has to). It is from these figures that they take their understandings of political events, of political figures and, in a broader sense, their understanding of what politics itself even is.[11] In this context, to know something about politics is to know something about these things—the traditional figures and institutions of political life.

This process acts like a magnifying glass under the hot sun, taking in a wide spectrum of light and concentrating it on a much smaller spot. We need to be alert to *who* is doing the filtering in these cases: Who holds the magnifying glass? The answer here is quite simple—those same traditional figures and institutions of political life who become the focus of attention are also the ones doing the focusing. In this sense, they are not only the performers but also the writers, commissioners, and broadcasters.

The result of this is that the dominant—by which I mean most influential—understanding of what it means to know something about politics is limited, focusing heavily on the goings on inside and around these traditional institutions and of those who inhabit them. In January 2020, Matt Chorley, a lead presenter for Times Radio (the radio wing of center-right newspaper *The Times*), tweeted some polling commissioned by his program on the station that was undertaken by opinion polling company, YouGov.[12] The polling purported to show that "most people have no idea what politicians are talking about" and was presented under the heading "Do You Speak Politicalese?" As part of the polling exercise, respondents were presented with a series of terms and asked whether they had heard of and understood each in a political context. So far, so good. The terms chosen, however, presumably by Chorley and others working on his radio program, provide an insight into their understanding of what it means to know something about politics—to speak politicalese. And their understanding matters as, for better or worse, Chorley and others like him are employed by traditional media outlets to discuss and explain politics with and to the general public.

The terms are a mish-mash of things including policies ("UBI", also known as "Universal Basic Income"), job titles of individuals in government ("SpAd", or "Special Advisor"), zeitgeisty media obsessions ("culture war"), and, eccentrically, a term from a speech by Winston Churchill ("sunlit uplands").[13] Far from measuring whether someone knows about politics, this has the whiff of a pub quiz about it. Indeed, the one thing it probably does measure is whether somebody is a political journalist or, heaven forbid, a politics geek. This is well-intentioned fun content for a radio show. Nonetheless, it is telling—letting us behind the curtain, Chorley is giving us an insight into what he, and those in roles similar to his, think it means to know something about politics. And, it turns out, this is knowing some words that politicians have said, some policies that have been hyped in the papers, and some bullshit phrases that float around political life like debris in floodwater.[14]

Casting an eye across some of the most cited—and therefore most influential—academic accounts of political knowledge in the discipline of political science, we can see a similar pattern. For example, one paper from the early 1990s, cited almost a thousand times at the time of writing, focuses mostly on the numbers of members of Congress drawn from each party ("Do you happen to know which party had the most members in the House of Representatives in Washington before the election this/last month?"), the division of powers laid out in the US Constitution ("Whose responsibility is it to determine if a law is constitutional or not ... is it the president, the Congress, or the Supreme Court?") and who holds which government jobs ("Do you happen to know what job or political office is now held by (insert name of current vice president?").[15] Similar questions can be seen in European variants, questions seeking to explore differences in political knowledge between men and women, and in the British Election Study.[16] It is not a stretch to say that these sorts of questions are the norm, and an accepted one at that, when it comes to establishing whether somebody knows something about politics. But what is accrued by knowing these things and being able to accurately recall them upon request? What is their relationship to the fundamentals of what it means to think about politics?

Passing the Test

The process that decrees what knowledge counts as political knowledge will, to a great extent, also decree who has it. This is reliant on the right sort of knowledge being identified by those administering the test: if you turned up at a driving test saying that you were very good at driving on Grand Theft Auto but less handy in a real life car, you wouldn't expect to pass.[17] If, however, you are seen to have the right kind of knowledge in politics, you and your ideas are more likely to get attention (mainly in the media) and, in many cases, some kind of credibility among those with some degree of power. Credibility matters, affecting who is listened to and who gets to speak into the loudest, most established microphones. If you aren't allowed near those microphones you might try making your own, something we have seen in recent years as a number of alternative news and information sources, carrying a variety of sometimes out there views and voices, enter the political sphere. Often these have had borderline catastrophic consequences, giving rise to concerns about fake news and misinformation among many observers. In many cases these concerns are justified—some sources are simply idiotic and should be treated as such. In other cases, however, it is true to say that the general thrust of the viewpoints being expressed via these alternative sources has some validity. Some offer a critique of politics, society, and the economy that is perhaps overlooked by mainstream outlets. (Indeed, we could even see the very existence of these alternative outlets as a response to the blind spots of the legacy media.)

The dominant narrative about political knowledge outlined above (that most people lack it) is one in which knowledge is demonstrated by knowing a lot about what is already the case— existing politicians and political institutions. Consequently, the kinds of knowledge that gain attention (and any associated credibility) will tend to be drawn from that same space, which in turn has the effect of reproducing the same ideas about politics in a kind of groupthink. This doesn't operate just on the level of thinking the same things about, say, specific policy solutions, but also operates on the level of baseline assumptions about what politics is, what it can achieve, and who should be involved in it. Political scientists have undertaken research that exposes some of the mistaken thinking this can lead to. One example is that journalists have been shown biased perceptions of public opinion, seeing it as more right-wing than it actually is. This has the resultant effect that focusing on right-wing narratives in the popular discussion of politics is seen as more acceptable than doing the opposite. We are thus less likely to move beyond where we already are.[18]

The dominant story about political knowledge has led to an idea taking hold—an idea that often takes the form of an assertion—that most people simply aren't interested in politics and do not wish to be. The former British Prime Minister, Tony Blair, encapsulated this view in his autobiography: "The single hardest thing for a practicing politician to understand is that most people, most of the time, don't give politics a first thought all day long . . . For most normal people, politics is a distant, occasionally irritating fog."[19] This kind of narrative can have real-world implications, not only in terms of who is encouraged to get involved in politics and the kinds of politicians we as citizens are expected to accept as suitable, but also in terms of who should be permitted to participate at all.

This narrative does the legwork of establishing a set of credentials that are deemed desirable—even essential—in order to participate in political decision-making. Explicit advocates of this position argue against widespread political participation on the basis that most people are epistemically underequipped to join in the making of political decisions. A notable example is that of the philosopher Jason Brennan. Brennan, and others who have written along similar lines like Bryan Caplan, makes the case that since most voters are ill-informed about public policy, are susceptible to cognitive biases that impede rational thinking, and are prone to misunderstand what is in their best interests, it would be just to limit participation in political decision-making to a select group of citizens who have shown themselves to be above average in performance across these kinds of metrics.[20] By way of example, Caplan suggests giving more votes to individuals or groups who display high levels of economic knowledge and the cessation of efforts to increase voter turnout. Brennan suggests doing this via a voter education assessment of some sort. At the same time, however, he acknowledges that this would likely exclude many of society's most vulnerable groups:

If the United States were to start using a voter qualification exam right now, such as an exam that *I* got to design, I'd expect that the people who pass the exam would be disproportionately white, upper-middle- to upper-class, educated, employed males. The problem here isn't that I'm racist, sexist, or classist . . . Instead, the problem would be that there are underlying injustices that tend to make it so that some groups are more likely to be knowledgeable than others. My view is rather than insist everyone vote, we should *fix* those underlying injustices. Let's treat the disease, not the symptoms.[21]

Brennan bases this assertion on a robust body of evidence showing that political knowledge correlates negatively with poverty, social exclusion, being an ethnic or racial minority, being a woman, and being young.[22] In Scott Althaus's study of US public opinion and collective preferences, he finds that individuals with lower levels of education, women, Blacks, those under the age of thirty-four, the financially worse-off, renters, and those living in urban areas are all underrepresented in the highest political knowledge quartile relative to their numbers in the overall population.[23] He writes that "knowledge of politics tends to be concentrated among those who are politically and socially advantaged."[24] These findings are replicated across time and space—essentially, being anything other than a rich, educated, white man puts one at a disadvantage in terms of the possession of political knowledge of the kind that a voter qualification exam would test.[25]

   The framing of politics adopted by Brennan and Caplan, among others, sees it as an activity that one can get "right" or "wrong" and, therefore, something in which acumen can be straightforwardly identified. Brennan does this by reducing political ability to tests on questions of knowledge of political institutions or constitutional procedure, and Caplan by reducing politics to questions of economic expertise—they use the dominant narrative. On this view there is a political realm, and those in the know have identified the kinds of relevant credentials to participate in it. Even if we jettison the idea of a test and allow people to participate regardless of demonstrable epistemic prowess, the assumption remains that there is an identifiable set of epistemic qualities that can be distributed evenly or unevenly across the population.

As is becoming clear, a lot turns on the question of which kinds of knowledge are deemed to be relevant to politics in particular, something which in turn rests on your views as to exactly what any fixed construction of "politics" as an activity is.

What Is Political About Politics?

I am skeptical that the dominant narrative, and any voter qualification exams it might spawn, measures political knowledge in a way that does justice to the idea of politics itself, or to individuals engaged in activities that are political in a way that doesn't fit neatly into the boxes prescribed by these survey questions. It is clear that these formulations have a bias toward knowledge-that—a knowledge of a series of propositions—when establishing what it means to know something about politics. But more than just the type of knowledge that is privileged, it is worth reiterating again the *focus* of these propositions—Congress, high-level policy discussion, the utterances of politicians. In many ways it is this, the focus, that is the issue I want to dwell further on here.

As a teenager, high off my first encounter with Richard Dawkins's *The God Delusion*, I recall robustly protesting my mother's request that I attend church on a Sunday morning with the rejoinder that I didn't need to go there to worship God, because "God is everywhere." As with God and church, a similar dispute arises when we ask where politics is happening. And the question of *where* directly stems from the question of *what* politics is—we can only see it happening if we are looking for it in certain places at all.

I have resisted a prescriptive definition of politics, not least because my aim in this chapter and this book as a whole is to drive home the idea that politics is sort of everything and therefore open to myriad interpretations. Nonetheless, considering some old and new definitions highlights their expansiveness. One of the most famous definitions of politics comes from Harold Laswell, who sees politics as "who gets what, when, how."[26] Andrew Gamble highlights how Aristotle and Cicero valued politics in the form of "speaking and acting in the public arena" and "the possession and employment of knowledge in practical affairs."[27] Gamble's own definition describes politics in terms of a process and an outcome: "Creating and sustaining a civil and political order which maintains civility by keeping conflict between its citizens within limits and guarantees certain liberties is a remarkable achievement whenever and wherever it occurs." He goes on to say that "there is more to politics than the occasionally bizarre and self-seeking behavior of some politicians ... politics is everywhere. It underpins the lives we lead."

We could go on examining definitions for some time (the supply is generous), but even this handful serve to demonstrate what we might see as the looseness of politics, a looseness that has the effect of making it almost omnipresent.[28] There is a sense that politics is closer to home than the kinds of survey measures described above would credit. These definitions change the focus of what it might mean to know something about politics, gesturing at issues and ideas that are perhaps more fundamental in nature than legislative seat distribution or who is the Senate majority leader.

Some of these definitions dwell on things that might even be better classified as knowledge-how—speaking and acting and the employment of knowledge in practical affairs. So, taken together, we can see these definitions of politics both broadening the span of what might be considered politics, growing beyond the focus on traditional institutions and actors outlined earlier, and also ending the monopoly of knowledge-that. These definitions open the door to the possibility that knowing something about politics may consist in the ability to do certain things and demonstrate certain practical abilities. Given the generalized nature of these abilities, it is difficult to imagine that they are not spread fairly widely across the population and not, as it were, the sole preserve of those in political institutions. And yet the dominant way that political knowledge has been measured in existing studies as "the range of factual information about politics that is stored in long-term memory" fails to reflect this.[29]

We might think this is symptomatic of a broader aversion to admitting that political knowledge could be more than propositional knowledge. In such a case, it might simply be that even if this standard doesn't quite do justice to the complexity of political knowledge, it picks up the most important parts. This defense might, however, be more convincing if a large chunk of political reporting didn't demonstrate such a preoccupation with the supposed know-how of the politicians we actually have in office. The briefest of considerations of the press coverage of leading political figures demonstrates that acknowledgment of the know-how of this group is a luxury not afforded to most.[30]

For example, the *Telegraph*'s Charles Moore, discussing the last-minute Brexit deal secured by Boris Johnson, wrote, "Boris has got us out, enormously assisted by enemies in his own party and outside too angry to perceive his skills."[31] Similarly, when Johnson released a video message following his release from hospital after suffering acute symptoms of COVID-19, the *Independent*'s John Rentoul wrote, "Like him or not, he is good at what he does... Boris Johnson is back with a video message of subtle political skill."[32]

A deeper sign of this willingness, even eagerness, to focus on know-how among political leaders is the political class' adoration of Robert Caro's four-volume (to date) biography of President Lyndon Baines Johnson. No doubt part of their fondness for Johnson's story is the simple notion that although unpopular in his time, history has looked more fondly upon him. This must be a tempting idea for politicians in office at a time when their stock could hardly sink lower. But the core of Caro's account of Johnson focuses on his skills as a legislator—understanding the rules, working at the edges of them, and combining this understanding with personal traits of both personality and physiology that made him effective at achieving his goals. Sure, Johnson knew the rules of the US Senate (propositional knowledge), but it was his skill at using that knowledge, his know-how, that made him more than just someone who was good at quizzes. It is perhaps that tantalizing prospect, that Caro has unearthed the nugget of know-how that transformed Johnson into a political titan, that has led the likes of former Leader of the Conservative Party, William Hague, to choose one volume of the biography as his desert island book.[33] (Self-improvement for the politician who doesn't achieve greatness themselves but likes the idea of it all the same.)

An obvious point to raise here is that these sound like fairly generic skills that are not only present outside of Westminster or DC, but actively honed outside of them too. What is political about the ability to negotiate deals or to speak clearly and convincingly or make judgment calls with some success? Selling your shares in a company at the right moment. Negotiating a pay rise with your boss. Addressing a neighborhood watch meeting. What's the difference? Where is the politics?

We could say that there is something to doing these things in the public eye that is missing in other cases, but this doesn't quite stand up in an age where celebrities regularly become advocates, often good advocates, for one issue or another that would traditionally be the preserve of elected politicians.[34] This is even true of members of the public who rise to prominence in the wake of some event, such as the cases of young people who survive school shootings becoming public advocates for gun control. And while the institutional context of formal politics is generally not replicated in other areas of life—specifically the fact that the whole enterprise is underpinned by principles and mechanisms of democratic accountability—this doesn't change the skills involved in dealing with those institutions or the other people within them. We might argue that the scale of the kinds of activity pursued in formal politics matters, but this hardly convinces when one considers that Facebook has, at the time of writing, 2.7 billion users and is ultimately controlled by a single individual, something true of a large number of other highly influential corporations. Similarly, we might say that the uniqueness lies in the convincing of so many others to take certain actions and to be able to enforce that with some legitimacy—this is perhaps most convincing, but this also happens in large organizations and among workforces of significant sizes. (To some degree, employees, shareholders, and customers take on the role of voters in this comparison.)

Ultimately it is hard to see what is different about political skill or leadership except the explicitly political nature of it—that is, what the *political* aims of any given politician are. Why did they get into political life in the first place? And why pursue these aims in politics and not, say, in the business or cultural worlds? This, of course, is the very thing that Rentoul is asking us to dismiss ("like him or not"). The claim, then, that there is such a thing as knowing something about politics that comes in the form of knowledge-how only seems to hold water if the actual politics involved is sidelined. Such a claim retains plausibility only if we detach this know-how, this skill, from what it is that is being done in concrete terms or, indeed, if we accept that politics only happens in a small number of designated places.

I am not saying that ordinary people, those who are not politicians, only possess political knowledge to the extent that they are able to do the things that politicians can. Rather, the point is that what the politicians are doing is nothing special! To some extent, the narrative about political skill (political know-how) reveals a slippage from thinking about politics as a vehicle through which power does its work in society to thinking about politics as simply what those with power do—a move from considering the effects of a social phenomenon to instead focusing on the actions of individuals in a place. In June 2020, a few months after he took on the role of leader of the Labour Party, Keir Starmer was praised by one political historian in the following terms:

> Starmer can chair a meeting. He can draft a minute. He can lead a team. He can hold a press conference. He can liaise with different offices. He can stay calm in an interview. Those skills look simple, but they're not.[35]

While not necessarily simple, these skills are unlikely to be especially rare. What is rare here, and thus what is worthy of note, is that they are skills possessed by a powerful person who works as a politician, something that most people do not do. Is this fact in itself enough to make the skills themselves political, though? And, at the same time, does it mean that this kind of political knowledge— political know-how—is, by definition, something that cannot exist elsewhere?

They Can't Say That They Haven't Been Warned

On June 14, 2017, an electrical fault in a refrigerator caused a fire to break out in a flat in Grenfell Tower, a twenty-four-story block in Kensington, West London. In the hours that followed the fire scaled the outside walls of the building, eventually resulting in the deaths of seventy-two residents who largely remained in their homes during the blaze. They remained in place because they had been told to do so by the authorities who assumed, incorrectly, that the nature of the design and construction of the block would isolate any fire within the flat it originated from. This was the worst residential fire in the UK since the Second World War. In the months following the tragedy, accounts emerged from residents showing that they had been highlighting fire safety issues for multiple years prior to the fire, sharing their concerns with their landlord, Kensington and

Chelsea Tenant Management Organisation (KCTMO). Collating and recording instances of neglected and deficient fire safety equipment they could see around the building, less than a year prior to the fire the residents prophetically wrote on their website, "[We] predict that it won't be long before the words of this blog come back to haunt the KCTMO management and we will do everything in our power to ensure that those in authority know how long and how appallingly our landlord has ignored their responsibility to ensure the heath [sic] and safety of their tenants and leaseholders. They can't say that they haven't been warned!"[36]

Sometimes we will have good reason to disregard certain information that is given to us and even to disregard people that we think are telling us information that is misleading or of no use. There is a risk, though, that in doing so we disregard the wrong information and potentially the wrong people. It can be hard to know who to believe. This question of who to listen to takes on greater importance when it is asked by those in a position of power. In the case of Grenfell, warnings were given and they were not taken heed of by those in power and the consequences were dire. The Grenfell disaster happened for reasons other than the fact that issues reported by residents were not acted on, but the incident offers a lens through which we can consider a bigger question that floats above contemporary politics. This is the question of what kind of knowledge is considered relevant by those in positions of power and what kind is not, which in turn brings us to a second, related question: that of who is listened to by those in power and who, on the contrary, is not.

The philosopher Miranda Fricker has developed an influential way of thinking about both of these questions, the concept of "epistemic injustice." She uses the term to refer to instances where "a wrong [is] done to someone specifically in their capacity as a knower."[37] By this she means that somebody is treated unjustly in terms of the kind of knowledge they possess and their ability to transmit this knowledge to others. There are two aspects to epistemic injustice on Fricker's account. First is something that she calls testimonial injustice:

> *Testimonial injustice* occurs when prejudice causes a hearer to give a deflated level of credibility to a speaker's word . . . an example . . . might be that the police do not believe you because you are Black.

These testimonial injustices will reflect existing inequalities in society. So, for example sexism will be embodied in cases of testimonial injustice where women's word is not taken as seriously as men's and racism in cases where the contributions of individuals from ethnic minorities are devalued. Fricker links this to the workings of two kinds of power. First is the unequal distribution of social power across society, social power defined by her as "a practically socially situated capacity to control others' actions, where this capacity may be exercised (actively or passively) by particular social agents, or alternatively, it may operate purely structurally."[38] Second is the work of what she calls *identity power*. Identity power comes into play "whenever there is an operation of power that depends in some significant degree upon such shared imaginative conceptions of social identity." In these cases, shared constructions of a given identity will affect how people assess what they hear other individuals say. Identity power relies on the work that shared ideas about certain social groups does in the background of society. In this sense, we do not need to consciously hold the belief that women are less rational than men, or that Blacks lie more than whites, for the underlying relations of identity power to take hold in a given situation. By way of example, earlier on I discussed the role that accents can play in social life, either allowing people to adapt and blend in to some contexts while making others stand out. If a society has a shared assumption that people who speak with a certain accent are likely to be less educated than people who speak with a different accent, this will affect how others perceive and assess what that person says, regardless of the merits (or otherwise) of what it is that they actually said. To put it more concretely, if someone in the UK speaks with an accent that sees them drop t's from their words—something considered improper by general elocutional standards—listeners are going to downgrade their assessment of what that person is saying. And, crucially, this can mean that they miss out on some potentially relevant piece of knowledge as a result, owing to either a conscious or unconscious prejudice against the source—say, for example, a blog written by residents of a tower block.[39]

It is not just the way that knowledge is expressed that matters here, but also the scope of what is considered relevant or even acceptable in terms of a contribution. When political knowledge focuses on the issues, forms, and sources that are deemed appropriate within the boundaries of the dominant narrative, things are missed. In the case above, the daily lived experience of Grenfell residents had provided them with knowledge regarding the likely unsafe fire equipment and recommended procedures in place at the building. It was foremost experiential knowledge, knowledge derived from the subjective perspective of what it was like to live in the tower itself.

Why is it, then, that this kind of knowledge is essentially absent from the dominant narrative about what political knowledge is and how we can establish who has it? The second aspect of Fricker's idea of epistemic injustice can go some way to explaining why we end up thinking about politics this way. This is the concept of hermeneutical injustice:

> *Hermeneutical injustice* occurs at a prior stage, when a gap in collective interpretive resources puts someone at an unfair disadvantage when it comes to making sense of their social experiences.[40]

Hermeneutical injustices occur when groups are marginalized from the process of creating shared hermeneutical resources—those "collective social understandings" that allow us to make sense of the world around us.[41] When we become aware that something is happening to us—for example, how we are being treated by some other group or institution—and we move to articulate to ourselves what is happening, we will find that we are coming up short; we don't have the language for it. This is an inability to label some experience that we have. More recently, philosophers have identified how hermeneutical injustice also manifests as a failure in our ability to properly assess those experiences: if we cannot appropriately label something that is going on in our lives, we will also be unable to properly place it in context and consider its implications for others in a similar position.[42] If we are impeded from seeing the fact that our protestations regarding the safety of the building in which we live are in fact instances of discrimination, we will be unable to get the word out about what has happened to others who may either be in a similar position or in a position to help. In other words, the political aspect of the experience (that aspect involving solidarity, power, and redress) will be dulled.

Critical to this, then, is the extent to which an individual is in a position where they can take part in the generation of collective social concepts—who decides what counts as discrimination, or whether the knowledge generated by living in a building is just as important as the perspective of a property developer when it comes to assessing fire safety precautions? Who decides what counts as politics? Viewing the production and use of these shared understandings as precisely that—the outcome of a process—allows us to see them

as reflecting the perspectives of different social groups, and to entertain the idea that relations of unequal power can skew shared hermeneutical resources so that the powerful tend to have appropriate understandings of their experiences ready to draw on as they make sense of their social experiences, whereas the powerless are more likely to find themselves having some social experiences through a glass darkly, with at best ill-fitting meanings to draw on in the effort to render them intelligible.[43]

This issue of looking for politics in the wrong places is an issue of hermeneutical injustice—of how the listener (or group of listeners) is constructing, and conceiving of, politics as an activity. For if we are to accept that there is an activity that we can confidently call "politics" and epistemic goods that are certain to be useful in its pursuit on this basis, we must surely then question *why* we have arrived at this conclusion and, perhaps more importantly, *who* got us there. It is entirely possible, maybe even inevitable, that any settled definition of a collective concept is going to be an expression of power. Indeed, Fricker argues that we can see how influence over the concept of politics can extend even to the collective identity that certain social groups will have in relation to that concept:

> We can imagine an informally disenfranchised group, whose tendency not to vote arises from the fact that their collectively imagined social identity is such that they are not the sort of people who go in for political thinking and discussion. "People like us aren't political"; and so they do not vote.[44]

Given what we know about the composition of political institutions in a broad sense—legislatures, parties, political media, and so on—and broader power structures in society, we can say with a great deal of certainty that many of the voices that would epistemically marginalized are not going to have, or have had in the past, much of a role in the generation of dominant collective conceptions of the activity of politics. If political knowledge is pub quiz trivia, we would do well to ask: Who is the quizmaster?

Life Itself

Over time, the idea that what people know about politics might be captured by a battery of generic questions about prominent political institutions and figures has become harder to sustain and consequently some political scientists have tried to move beyond this by adopting alternative measures of political knowledge. For example, studies have explored whether women are better at answering questions about politics that focus on elements of the political system that might be more relevant to women—the numbers of women in political institutions,[45] or the names of prominent women politicians,[46] and find that women are, overall, likely to demonstrate higher levels of knowledge when these gendered measures are used compared to the generalized ones discussed previously.

Other studies have sought to establish whether or not people are now more likely to hold issue-specific political knowledge in place of generalized knowledge—being able to recite the policy positions of prominent politicians on specific issues that they care about, like reproductive rights or gun ownership, for example (answer: they do, but they often take information from extreme sources, potentially contributing to an increase in single-issue voting).[47] Another innovative study of political knowledge among US citizens considered the possibility that different people would have different kinds of knowledge that divide across two dimensions.[48] The first dimension distinguishes, like the studies noted above, between general knowledge and policy-specific knowledge. The second dimension, however, considered the temporality of political knowledge—that is, how long has the fact in question been around? On this dimension, the authors highlight a distinction between "static" facts (those that have existed for some time) and "surveillance" facts (those that change and, to be known accurately, would require an individual to keep up to date with ongoing political events). They found that higher levels of education were associated with sizable increases in respondents' ability to answer general questions about politics of both the static and surveillance variety, but less so with policy questions of either kind. And in terms of the impact of consuming media coverage of political events, respondents exposed to high amounts of news coverage only had a higher probability of correctly responding to general surveillance questions—those regarding ongoing political events. Simply consuming a greater volume of news coverage had no apparent effect on respondents' ability to correctly answer traditional questions about political institutions or about policy (this was true across both static and surveillance question types). To put this another way, exposing oneself to more news coverage of politics might give you a better sense of who is up and who is down on a given day, but it will increase neither your knowledge of political institutions nor your understanding of public policy. In other words, you might perform better on the radio quiz I discussed earlier, but that's about it.

Political scientists have also considered the possibility that differences in motivation will affect the kind of political knowledge citizens possess. The thought is that people will be more likely to seek out knowledge that matters to them, knowledge they are more likely to either need or to use. For example, it remains the case that in the US, Black citizens are far more likely to encounter the carceral face of the state, with Black men proportionally the most jailed group in American society and Black citizens more likely to deal with the police. Under these circumstances, the way that Black Americans interact with the state will be more likely to involve the justice system, broadly defined, than we would expect for the average white citizen. A recent study sought to establish whether this imbalance was reflected in the kind of political knowledge possessed by Black citizens, namely whether African Americans exhibited greater knowledge of the carceral state compared to whites.[49] In addition to asking respondents the traditional political knowledge questions described earlier (e.g., which party dominated the legislative branch), the authors also included questions asking respondents to identify six recent victims of police violence that had received more or less prominence in the media.[50] To put this in terms of the study mentioned above, this measures political knowledge of the surveillance kind, but within a specific policy area. Perhaps unsurprisingly, the authors' study suggested that African Americans were significantly more likely to possess knowledge of who the victims of carceral state violence were than whites. Conversely, white respondents were better able to answer the traditional political knowledge questions than African American respondents.

Motivation to obtain certain knowledge may, then, be a question of necessity as in the case above, but it could also be a simple question of interest. For some time, it was accepted among political scientists that women had lower levels of political knowledge than men, with multiple studies using traditional survey questions to establish this across time and place. Recent years, however, have brought a recognition that the way in which questions are asked, and what they are asked about, affects the existence and nature of this apparent gender gap in political knowledge.[51] The theory behind these studies stems from statistics showing that women are more likely to use a range of government services than men, primarily as a result of the fact that women are more likely to take on caring responsibilities of all kinds. As such, scholars have hypothesized that asking women about aspects of political life considered to be more relevant to them—that is, about those services that women are more likely to use than men, services somehow connected to caring responsibilities—may nullify any gender difference in political knowledge identified using traditional questions.

This is a question of where we look (and thus what we look for) when trying to establish who knows what about politics. On what are we focusing our magnifying glass? Dietlind Stolle and Elizabeth Gidengil, analyzing data from Canadian respondents, find that the gender gap in political knowledge essentially disappears when political knowledge is measured by asking people about these practical elements of political life—for example, how government benefits work and what the state can offer in terms of specific support services.[52] As Stolle and Gidengil note, political scientists generally do not study citizen understanding of these kinds of government programs when examining levels of political knowledge, something that seems strange considering that interaction with these programs is part of the fabric of people's actual daily lived interactions with (the product of) political processes. In reality people are more likely to use a government service than they are to meet the Speaker of the House of Representatives. As Stolle and Gildengil put it, women's "political engagement often blurs the lines between what has traditionally been considered the public and private spheres."

Across these studies, we can see a move toward considering people's experiences as sources of not only useful knowledge, but as something that can generate political knowledge. The focus of the magnifying glass is expanding. Summarizing this work, Katherine Cramer and Benjamin Toff identify a category of experiential (political) knowledge that is transmitted through "stories about one's own experience with a policy, a political actor, or interactions with government or other individuals and groups."[53] They argue that "when we are assessing the competence of citizens, we need to do more than look at the quantity or even quality of political information they possess." Studying a Wisconsin rural community's participation in race relation dialogues in addition to a series of interviews with political journalists and operatives, Cramer and Toff found that essentially everybody uses their own personal experience as a way to frame what they know about politics. More than this, they found that people used experience as a way of connecting with other people, seeking to understand why they thought about political issues the way that they did by listening to their experiences. As the authors put it, when people talk about politics in this way, "they are not only making sense of issues, they are sharing themselves."

When knowledge is so wedded to, and rooted in, experience, and possession of it becomes a necessity of navigating the social world one is presented with, is this not more akin to an ability? Is it not the case that this is less about your knowledge *of* something and more about knowing how to do it? How to navigate the world, navigate one's reality? Is this, too, not politics? For most of us, the meat of politics is our ability to do this kind of thing—it isn't knowing about parliamentary procedure or who holds what ministerial office; it is life itself.

3

Think About Presence

Immense Responsibility

In November 2018, four women were elected to the US House of Representatives. In and of itself, this simple fact was, by 2018, not that unusual. But in other ways these women were unusual, seemingly out of kilter with the institution they had entered. By the standards of the US Congress they were young, with an average age of less than forty. They were all from minority backgrounds: African American, Latinx, and Somali American. Two became the first Muslim women ever elected to Congress. Indeed, the group was seen as so remarkable that collectively they gained a nickname, "The Squad," and one of their number, Alexandria Ocasio-Cortez, became a fully fledged celebrity: star of a Netflix documentary, followed by 12.6 million people on Twitter, and possessor of an instantly recognizable nickname ("AOC"). Soon after her election, Ocasio-Cortez gave an indication of the level of hype around her rise to political notoriety: "I turned around this corner to get on the street and this woman saw me and just started crying. She just broke down crying. And even though I didn't feel like a different person, I felt this immense responsibility of all of these people's hopes and dreams for our future."[1]

Traditionally, political representation was thought of largely in terms of ideas, with little attention given to who was actually present in the relevant institutions. There was an assumption that so long as a certain range of thought was expressed within political institutions—thought corresponding to the major schools of conservatism and liberalism and socialism—it didn't matter that much

How to Think about Politics. Peter Allen, Oxford University Press. © Oxford University Press (2025).
DOI: 10.1093/9780197679395.003.0004

who it was that was doing the expressing. Ideas trumped presence. But over time, as white men continued to dominate political institutions well into the twentieth century, this traditional account was brought into question. Critics asked whether it really was the case that anybody could accurately and effectively speak for the increasingly diverse groups of people who lived in advanced democracies. And when the numbers of women and minorities in politics slowly grew, the difference they made to the decisions that political institutions made suggested that it wasn't; it really did seem to matter who was present.

The Squad were emblematic of the good news story that we have been in a position to tell about political representation in recent decades. In entering Congress, and by being young minority women, The Squad showed that it is possible (even increasingly normal) to have people from a broader slice of society in the places where decisions are made. They let us tell a positive story about presence and, arguably, about politics itself. That story has convincing evidence to point to: in the last decade and a half, we have had the first Black president of the US, the first British-Asian and the second (and, fleetingly, third) woman prime minister of the UK.

But the positive story isn't the only story. Part of the puzzle of the kinds of representative advances that many democracies have seen is that they have been, to many, something of a disappointment. Although there have been clear gains in one sense, in many other ways the kinds of political transformations that some might have expected these previously inconceivable events to bring about have simply not materialized. In 2022 the US Supreme Court overturned *Roe v. Wade*, removing a woman's constitutional right to an abortion. The 2016 election of Donald Trump saw an outright sexist enter the most powerful office in the world notwithstanding the exposure of his comments about grabbing women "by the pussy." Indeed, this same man received 41 percent of his votes from women.[2] Globally, the rise of far-right political parties has seen a backlash against progressive policies that broadly expanded or secured the rights of women, gays and lesbians, ethnic minorities, and others who had been largely frozen out of political life (frozen out of presence). In fact, it is often the political parties who worked hardest to bring these groups into politics in the first place (mainstream center-right and center-left parties) who are now cutting them loose in an attempt to stem the flow of votes away from the political center.[3]

What is going on? Despite the increasing prominence of representational logic across industries as different as the media, financial services, and the legal industry, it feels like the core idea underpinning this logic—that a greater diversity among those present in various spheres of public life will transform those spheres for the better—exists under a perennial Sword of Damocles; the sword in this case being the moment when its proponents realize that maybe representation wasn't where the action was after all. They bought the sizzle but they're still waiting for the steak. Presence matters, then, that much is clear. But were we—and are we still—asking too much of it?

A Solution to a Problem

The representation part of representative democracy is ultimately a solution to a problem. The problem? That societies wanted (some kind of) equality in the political sphere—everybody getting an equal say in the process of political decision-making—but could not achieve that goal by allowing everybody to actually have that say themselves. If you have too many people trying to have a say, you can't hear anyone. Logistically, it becomes difficult to design spaces and procedures that could facilitate direct democracy of this kind and at this scale.

In this context, representation offers a solution to the problem— it allows everybody to have an equal say in the political process not by actually having their say in literal terms, but by having an equal opportunity to choose others—representatives—who will speak on their behalf. In theory, we all get the same input into who comprises this smaller group that stand in our place and act on our behalf. Problem solved.

But solving one problem creates another.[4] Would it matter who these people were, these representatives? For a long time, the accepted answer was "no." Or, more accurately, for a long time that question wasn't asked in any serious way, an omission that owed its longevity largely to the fact that for most of the history of representative democracy the unquestioned norm was that the representatives would be men, mostly from racial majorities, and mostly from wealthier backgrounds. There are many reasons that this situation went largely unchallenged for long periods of time, but one key contributor was that the majority of the population in these representative democracies was not allowed to participate in the form of either voting or running for political office themselves. You can't ask a question if you aren't allowed to speak. And those who were allowed to choose representatives (primarily rich, white men) were perfectly content to perpetually choose other people like them (primarily rich, white men).

Over time, as these fledgling representative democracies became mass democracies, more citizens were allowed to help do the choosing and disparities between the choosers and the chosen became more conspicuous, rendering any pretense that the status quo lived up to democratic ideals of inclusion and equality harder and harder to maintain.[5] (If those who you are able to vote for bear no meaningful similarity to you, it is harder to imagine that they will do a good job of representing your views and interests.) Demands for improved representation in the form of a more proportional reflection of the wider population among elected representatives got louder over time.

Slowly, but generally steadily, those demands have been met in many advanced democracies. It is now highly unusual—even jarring—to see group photographs of leading politicians where all of the protagonists are men. This process would have occurred even more slowly if not for a range of methods adopted across various political systems with the explicit aim of speeding things up. Most notably, these have included the use of quotas of different kinds. Generally speaking, quotas serve to guarantee a certain outcome when it comes to either the selection or election of political candidates—at the selection stage, a quota will ensure that a political party chooses somebody from the group of the population who is the focus of the quota when deciding who they will put in front of voters, and at the election stage, a quota will guarantee that whomever is elected, they will be from the chosen group. Some quotas have been implemented voluntarily by political parties, others adopted under the force of legislation, and others have become part of their country's constitutions. (In total, over sixty countries have passed legislation requiring quotas of some kind.)

In this sense, the sickness was identified, the medicine administered, and the symptoms relieved. But the medicine's effectiveness did not mean that the whole endeavor proceeded without controversy. For some critics, quotas reduced the quality of politicians by letting in candidates who would not have been good enough to make it without the procedural leg up that the quota provided. For others, gender quotas focused on electing more women meant that men who had done their time in a local constituency, preparing the ground for their own candidacy, were now sidelined through no fault of their own, their own political careers ending without ever getting going. Further criticisms have been leveled that the women selected via these quotas perform less well at the ballot box (not the case) and then go on to be less effective in Parliament once elected (also not the case). In fact, it is not controversial to say that there is no statistical evidence that women selected for candidacy via a gender quota are that different at all to women selected through "normal" means, or indeed to the men that political parties select either.[6]

That said, quotas and their implementation do disrupt settled political practice in a way that some people could justifiably see as unfair. In systems where political parties have almost total control over candidate selection processes, individuals will dedicate years, sometimes decades, of their lives to doing the kinds of things that prospective candidates need to be seen to have done to have a shot at being among the chosen. This will include activities like campaigning for other party candidates by spending many (too many) weekend hours knocking on doors and delivering campaign literature to potential voters and dedicating evenings to "phone banking" for party candidates by calling unsuspecting members of the public on the telephone. It will include attending meetings with other activists to debate and decide on often arcane procedural matters of minor practical concern. If one was serious from a young age about their desire to enter politics, this seriousness may even preclude certain recreational activities (nobody wants an unwelcome photograph to come to light at just the wrong moment). All in all, getting to the position of being a credible contender for selection in a parliamentary seat is no small task in which you give a lot to (maybe) get a little.

As such, I do not think it is unreasonable for men—or members of any demographic sidelined by a quota—to feel somewhat put out when they hear that their party is implementing a gender quota in the seat where they have put in this legwork (bear in mind that in the UK, these selection processes increasingly favor so-called local candidates, so any currency that has been built up is not necessarily portable in geographic terms). What is unreasonable, however, is to weigh this individual cost against the collective purpose that gender quotas serve and see the two as equal. The error that creeps in here is to analyze a political event at one level at the expense of another. What do I mean by this? In this case, focusing on the (understandable) negative emotions of an individual man and his supporters in a single constituency means that we miss the wood for the trees. The wood, in this case, is the broader socio-political and historical context that has seen women effectively excluded from political institutions for most of the time these have existed. This is why quotas exist in the first place: to remedy this imbalance. If we were to generate a hypothetical unfairness-omometer to measure the total amount of unfairness (not to mention material disadvantage) felt by these women as a result of this exclusion, I am fairly confident it would outweigh that felt by the man and his supporters in that constituency. This may seem callous, and in general I would discourage such utilitarian thinking on political issues, but the fact is that these selections are zero-sum by nature (to increase the numbers of women, the numbers of men will have to decrease) and in this instance hurt feelings and stymied ambitions are, in democratic terms, worth the cost.

And there is progress. According to the United Nations, 26.5 percent of politicians elected to lower houses of Parliament worldwide are women as of January 2023, an increase of over 15 percent since the mid-1990s.[7] Globally, 28 women serve as head of state or government and women comprise 23 percent of all cabinet ministers worldwide. Among EU member states, this number stands at 33 percent.[8] Following the 2019 UK General Election, there are 66 MPs with ethnic minority backgrounds, this up from 4 in 1987 and 15 in 2005.[9] The 118th US Congress (first sitting in 2023) was the most racially diverse ever—indeed, each Congress since the 111th has been the most diverse ever, surpassing its predecessor.[10] The UK House of Commons has claimed the title of "most gay" legislature, with estimates that around 11 or 12 percent of MPs identify as LGBT+, a number that is steadily increasing. The same is true, albeit on a smaller scale, of the US Congress, where a record number of LGBT+ legislators sit in the 118th Congress.[11] Whichever indicator you choose, they tell a similar story. It is not a story of overwhelming and total success but political stories rarely are. Rather, it is a story of steady progress. The numbers look healthier and healthier—representation for historically marginalized groups is improving.[12] This is not to say that the situation is perfect or that political institutions operate on an equitable basis for all members (it isn't and they don't), but the numbers of women, LGBT+, and ethnic minority politicians in positions of power has grown to the point where the obvious next step is to ask whether this increase has brought about the changes many hoped it would.

Tilting the Scales

Perhaps predictably, there is no simple answer to this query. For some, the mere fact that the numbers have increased and that there are now more women, more minorities, and more LGBT+ politicians will itself suffice as evidence of representation having delivered change. Simply by virtue of being there, of being present, evidence suggests that these politicians offer symbolic change that matters to citizens.[13] The presence of members of a previously excluded group in a political institution (an institution, we should remind ourselves, that makes decisions about how society should be) can signal meaningful things to other members of that group in the population as whole, namely that members of that group are just as able to make consequential decisions about big issues as the groups that previously dominated political life. In places where those groups were actively forbidden from being involved in politics, for example Blacks in the United States, this will arguably matter all the more.[14] Katelyn E. Stauffer identified a neat way of testing this hypothesis in the case of women by asking American men and women about their own political efficacy (how politically influential and listened to they personally feel) alongside their estimate of the numbers of women elected to political office at the state and national level.[15] Next, Stauffer would correct their usually inflated estimates of the number of women politicians and found that in cases where participants had overestimated the presence of women, their political efficacy would decline based on the new, lower number. To put it another way, the more women that people—both men and women—thought there were in politics, the more politically efficacious they felt.

For others, evidence of change will come mainly in the form of material gains for that group—policy changes, institutional reforms, the remedying of historical wrongs or oversights.[16] These things would be meatier and, in theory, more identifiable, than less tangible (or at least less easy to grasp) symbolic effects. There is evidence that personal experience and identity guides the policymaking of individual politicians, with studies showing that the sexuality, race, social class, and gender of legislators seems to affect how they vote and advocate on different issues.[17] So, the evidence suggests that there is a difference made when the composition of our political institutions changes—for political scientists, this is the main element of interest. The fact that there is any change whatsoever tells us something about political institutions (what they do will depend, at least to a point, on who is in them) and about politicians (their life experiences seem to condition how they approach their work).[18]

However, not all of us are political scientists—for most of us, the fact that policy outputs change when there are more diverse representatives is potentially a fun fact, but it doesn't really *do* anything for us. We will want to know *what* the changes are, especially if we too are a member of one of those groups that has historically been underrepresented in political life. But even this gets tricky. For all of the societal groups that are attached to identities that we might care about (our gender, ethnicity, and so on), there exists a huge amount of heterogeneity among its members. Not all women agree what is best for women, neither do all men agree what is in men's interests.[19] The same is true of ethnic or racial groups, people from the same place or who are the same age, or even among people who identify themselves as part of the same social class.[20]

And yet despite this, the kinds of changes that take place do seem to trend toward making things better for those groups, broadly speaking. As Jane Mansbridge puts it, "the evidence now seems clear that once you look beyond roll call votes, Black legislators do a better job than Whites of representing Black constituents, women legislators do a better job than men of representing female constituents, and legislators from working-class backgrounds do a better job than others of representing working-class constituents."[21] Political theorists seeking to explain this outcome are understandably keen to avoid essentialism when discussing this connection between presence and outcomes. They do not want to be in the position of saying "things get better for women because there is some core element of womanhood that these women bring to politics that was previously missing."[22] There are ways to think about the connection that emphasize that there is clearly *something* shared by women, men, whites, Blacks, and so on that is not shared by individuals who are not in these groups and that thing is quite likely to be rooted in their experience of living in the world as members of those groups.[23] To put it another way, if the world treats you and others like you as members of a given gender or racial group, you will all know what this is like in some way that is common among you. Framing the connection in this way avoids essentialism (it is not saying there is some authentic core of gender or race) and instead focuses on how individuals may come to realize that their experiences of life, conditioned by gender and race, are shared in some way that may become politically relevant. Indeed, this is the logic that underpins collective political actions like strikes. (A famous example is the Grunwick strike at a film-processing plant in North London that took place in the late 1970s. The strikers ultimately lost their dispute, and their jobs, but the diversity of the workers involved meant that Grunwick became a point of reference whenever those on strike were not the classic white, slightly older men of popular imagination.)[24] Experiences don't need to be shared in their entirety to make a difference across multiple groups of people.

   The system works, then, to a greater or lesser extent. You change the composition—the input—of political institutions and out come different policies, policies that again to a greater or lesser extent, seem to be better for the people who previously looked to those institutions and saw few or no people who were like themselves. This sounds like a success story, which to some degree it is. But if you look around you at the state of political institutions in countries like Hungary, India, the US, and the UK and then consider the way that politics is conducted in those countries and after that think about the way that a lot of minorities in these places are treated even now, it doesn't *feel* like so much of a success story. There is a gap between what we might expect things to be like and what things are actually like.

Barack Obama, inaugurated as the 44th president of the United States in 2009, was the first African American to hold that office. Some commentators at the time saw this fact as evidence that America had become a "post-racial" society, no longer burdened by the historical legacies of slavery and countless other racist policies and, as scholars noted at the time, such a view chimed well with the opinions of white Americans who believed that African Americans had achieved racial equality.[25] The narrative was a positive story about America and Americans. The assumption, albeit an unspoken one, was that by being elected, Obama brought not only symbolic representation but also delivered the goods in material terms by drawing a line under the racist history of the US.

Writing a decade and a half after the event and sitting at the peak of Mount Hindsight, I know that this did not come to pass. While Obama himself is still reasonably popular (depending on who you ask) and arguably did make significant progressive moves in public policy terms (again, your mileage will vary depending on the audience), it is clear that the United States is far from being a post-racial country.[26] Indeed, it may even be further away from that (in whatever form you choose to imagine) than it was in 2009. All politicians leave complicated legacies, but Obama's feels more complicated than most owing to the emphasis placed on the representational gain that his election embodied. The source of this initial emphasis isn't especially relevant (it was coming from all angles), but it arguably left Obama, and the idea of presence itself, on the hook for a large bar tab that could not be paid.

Respect the Water

The last fifteen years or so have seen two things happen alongside one another. On the one hand, people have become more sensitive to the kinds of questions of presence I am talking about in this chapter. I think this is a good thing, for the most part—our politicians are generally increasingly diverse and greater emphasis is placed on these aspects of who our politicians are. Alongside this, material (read: financial) inequality has increased essentially everywhere, and has done so quickly.[27] People feel poorer while they see others getting richer.[28] The rent is too high, groceries cost too much, and wages are not rising as much as they should be. This material part of everyone's experience, everyone's identity, has asserted itself more and more and to many, it has become apparent that you cannot pay bills solely with an increased diversity of representation.

I do not say this to justify any backlash against efforts to diversify presence or suggest that this is somehow a luxury only to be pursued during better economic times, but rather I want to suggest a reason why the undoubted gains we have seen in terms of political representation are not translating to the kind of politics we thought they might. In other words, it is possible (and important) to offer an account of representation that acknowledges the limitations of various kinds that affect what it might be able to achieve.

It is not just economic inequality that is tilting the scales. Multiple political scientists have, in the last three decades or so, noted contradictions running to the very heart of how representative democracy functions that affect how citizens perceive its success or otherwise. One contention of this literature is that most of us are not very good at appreciating it when representative democracy actually does what we want it to. That is, we labor under the misapprehension that representation is not doing much for people like us when, in reality, it might be. Or, at least, it will be better than any alternative to democracy.[29] The risk is that by not remembering the grim reality of these alternatives, disappointment with actually existing representative democracy results in us having our heads turned by something flashier and seemingly novel, even if it is neither of these things.

Part of this stems from the fact that much contemporary politics runs to the duller side of things. We face huge, civilization-scale problems (e.g., climate change) but the solutions never seem to have a commensurate heft (e.g., not permitting certain cars to be driven in certain parts of certain cities at certain times). Contemporary politics is highly complex, something that can easily be misperceived as it being needlessly, deliberately, complicated and unresponsive. Dealing with these big issues means dealing with numerous institutions, in multiple places, that are interconnected in often messy ways. If a politician presses a figurative button in London or DC, it is not easy to predict how, if at all, this system will respond. Accounting for why things have got so complicated is like playing a round of buzzword bingo (globalization! technology! reform!) and the real answer is that it is the result of all of these things and others too. Watching from the outside, the whole thing can seem like a pointlessly finicky game that you are not being given a chance to understand.

But it is not the case that things are bewildering for those on the outside alone. Political institutions at all levels—town councils, state legislatures, government departments, national and international legislatures—are messy. Global networks can be too slow or too fast. The policies being designed to address certain issues are so complex that politicians themselves can barely understand the details of the laws they are being asked to approve. The consensus among scholars of the UK Parliament is that "without . . . the whips, most busy MPs would struggle to know which way to vote in the division lobbies."[30] There are obvious concerns to be raised about this situation, not least that it leaves politicians open to disproportionate influence from special interests who are able to "explain" the legislation to them in a way that best suits those special interests. Thinking in more democratic terms, it means it is difficult for politicians to explain to the public exactly what they have done and why. If this is opaque or difficult to follow, satisfaction is less likely to follow—it will have the feeling of an itch you cannot quite scratch. When this is happening not only in national Parliament but also at a supranational level through the constraints of trade agreements and international law, the complexity compounds.[31]

This sense of the dial being turned up to eleven has been identified by other scholars as an instance of "hyper-democracy," "neither 'more democracy' nor 'an excess of democracy' but 'the intensification' of democracy."[32] As a higher volume of demands are made of the political system, and more and more questions asked of it when it seems to be less and less responsive, politicians can appear impotent.[33] At the same time, politicians have played their own part in handing away decision-making power on a large number of issues. If we think that politicians are doing less (or seem able to influence less), we are to some extent correct. Political scientists refer to this as "depoliticization," the gifting of responsibility for decisions about a policy area from politicians to "unelected managers, professionals and experts."[34] This apparent lack of self-belief (not "backing yourself," as professional sportspeople say) means that big policy areas, in both literal and figurative terms, are not in the direct control of the people that most of us would think we elect to control them. Sometimes this borders on the absurd. In July 2023, the Shadow Chancellor the Exchequer in the UK, Labour politician Rachel Reeves, was asked by Sky News reporter, Sophy Ridge, for her view on the role of the Bank of England in the UK's ongoing economic woes, specifically their decision to raise interest rates. Reeves's response was that "we must respect economic institutions," by which she meant that it would not be proper for her to comment on the actions of the Bank.[35] Given that the interest rate rise had caused millions of Britons' mortgage payments to skyrocket and had brought the country to the edge of an economic recession, it does seem heavy with pathos that the person pitching themselves as the next Chancellor felt unable to say what they thought about this state of affairs.[36] Imagine a lifeguard, watching from the edge of the pool as you struggle, saying that we need to respect the water.

An interesting development in recent years has been the concurrent repoliticization of issues that had seemed to be more or less settled by public consensus or longstanding tradition. At the elite level, this might include Donald Trump bucking convention regarding the acceptance of the results of the 2020 presidential election. In a broader sense, it includes the rise of explicitly misogynistic figures in the public sphere, such as YouTuber Andrew Tate, and the labeling of a vast range of things as "woke" in an effort to discredit them. (In the week I am writing this, the UK's high speed rail program has been labeled as "woke" by tabloid media for reasons escaping understanding and the same fate has been met by the "15-minute city" movement, which is ultimately about how far one needs to travel to buy a loaf of bread.)[37]

People have always disagreed with their political opponents on matters of substance (who should get what, when, and how) but, so the claim goes, tribalism is different in that it is not about policy distance but rather is about how you feel about the other group in affective terms. On this, the evidence seems clear—more and more people dislike (or "loathe," as one study puts it) their political opponents.[38] In numerical terms, recent data from Pew suggests that around 9 in 10 registered voters thought that an electoral victory for the opposing side would result in "lasting harm" to the United States.[39] Politically diverse marriages (where spouses support different political parties) are on the decline in the United States.[40] Even Thanksgiving family dinners appear to be shorter where there are political differences among attendees than where there are not.[41] More seriously, polarization has taken physical form in incidents like the storming of the Capitol on January 6, 2021 and increasingly violent right-wing activity across other Western democracies.[42]

This affective polarization—feeling more emotionally engaged in politics in a way that is hostile to your political opponents—has also been shown to reduce what political scientists call "loser's consent" following elections.[43] Traditionally seen as a measure of how healthy a democracy is, loser's consent, as the name suggests, is the extent to which individuals accept that their side lost an election and assent to the other side taking power. The fact that this situation has existed for much of the time since the second world war in most advanced democracies led many of us to assume that it would continue to do so indefinitely. We were wrong.

In this situation, the stakes will feel higher for everybody involved. Disputes between activists will run warmer, with slights felt more keenly. Promises and rhetoric from politicians will slowly overheat with the consequence that nothing is ever quite enough anymore. In turn, this makes the next round of promises ever more grand (and ever less likely to come to fruition). By way of example, questions regarding the legacy of former senior politicians now split almost entirely along partisan lines, seemingly ruling out any sense of a fair hearing from the other side.[44] Being a representative must surely be more of a challenge under these conditions.

This challenge is indicative of what I see as a broader concern about the role of presence, of representation, in contemporary political life. A lot of the weight of the classic notion of representation depended on a certain degree of fixity and stability, even on the now revolutionary idea that people might do what they said they would do when they asked for your vote. For the most part, it used the idea of fixed constituencies, both geographically and in terms of identity, to draw the formal and informal boundaries that dictated who was responsible for doing what for whom: politicians

represented certain geographical areas and political parties represented the interests of certain sections of society, usually along the
lines of class. (I am simplifying things a touch here, but not too
much—class voting, usually conceived as the percentage of manual
workers voting for a left-wing party, peaked after the Second World
War and then declined over time, though it remained at a high
level until the 1990s depending on who you read.)[45] While politicians are still overwhelmingly elected by people living in a spatially
delimited place and then go on to represent that same place in the
legislature, this idea of "constituency" has become more messy over
time as cross-cutting claims to be representing different groups that
are not fixed in geographical place have become more common.

Most obviously, this has come as representation has diversified
but not uniformly in all places. For example, there are many more
African American Congresspeople now than 60 years ago, but this
does not mean that every single African American lives in a district
represented by an African American politician. In this situation
we might expect some benefits of symbolic representation to persist beyond the geographic border of the district in question but it
also seems to be the case that there are more tangible representative effects that also persist, something that Jane Mansbridge has
called "surrogate representation."[46] The political scientist David
Broockman conducted an experimental study of how likely legislators were to respond to people who wrote to them who had
putatively Black names.[47] He then randomly varied whether the
supposed letter writer lived in the legislator's district or not (i.e.,
were they actually a direct constituent?). When the correspondent
lived outside the district, non-Black legislators were less likely to
respond to them while Black legislators responded at roughly the
same rate regardless. Whatever representation is going on here, it
is not just symbolic (there is tangible assistance provided by the
politician) and it is equally not taking place within the boundaries
of any traditionally defined constituency.

This is not a bad thing, but it does complicate the link between
politician and constituent. If a Black citizen either is not, or feels

they are not, represented by their geographically defined representative, it is good that there is the option to petition a Black legislator in another district. At the same time, though, they can't reward that person by giving them their vote and they can't hold them to account by withholding it—accountability is essentially absent. (More prosaically, it is probably not sustainable in the longer run for Black legislators to be undertaking what is strictly extra, unresourced, work.)[48] Of course, something like this arrangement occurs for citizens whenever their own representative holds a different view to them on an issue of the day (a war, specific policy, or a moral issue) while another representative does not. Indeed, if you live in an area that essentially always votes the opposite way to you (that is, you are a Democrat living in a red state or vice versa), for you this kind of representation will be the only game in town. The hope is that in the round, a representative body will contain groups and views proportional to their overall numbers in the population being represented. The problem is that we do not live in the round or in aggregate. We live where we live and can only vote for the politicians put on the ballot paper in front of us. So while the system may well be working in some grander sense, it might not feel like it.

There are (arguably growing) constraints on what representation can deliver. All of these constraints make it harder to see representation getting the results we might want. But at the same time, we also see more and more demands for representation, which leaves us asking a simple question—to what end?

All These Blonde, Blue-Eyed Girls

On the day of the Women's World Cup Final in August 2023, commentators on Sky News UK were reviewing that day's newspapers. The *Sunday Mirror* had published a cover depicting six of the English women's soccer team (known as "The Lionesses"), wishing them luck in that day's final. During the discussion between the presenter and two commentators, a male commentator, entrepreneur Wilfred Emmanuel-Jones, said: "The only thing I would say about this picture here—what jumps out at you—this doesn't represent diverse Britain. It's all these blonde, blue-eyed girls and, you know, I wish them well but I do think we need to ask ourselves questions about why is it that we've got—that there's a lack of diversity . . . if the whole idea behind this is to encourage more women to go into the sport, you need some sort of representation there to say 'whatever background you come from, you could get to this sort of level.'"[49]

This kind of discussion, where the language of (political) representation is ported to a domain that is not explicitly political, is increasingly the norm. It is now common to see Hollywood studios discussed in this way, along with catwalk fashion shows, the corporate leadership of investment banks, and the media.[50] Specific films and television programs are critiqued on the basis of how they represent different groups.[51] Even the views held by fictional characters in novels are up for grabs when it comes to whether they represent certain viewpoints and the extent to which they do this in an acceptable way.[52]

The logic of representation—very roughly, the idea that diversity of representation of traditionally marginalized groups is a (capital G, capital T) Good Thing and will, in some way, bring about further Good Things—is now common in political, economic, and cultural domains. Broadly speaking, the unit of change in this argument is the individual—the solution to the ills of a lack of representation is presence. And presence will always, ultimately, be about bringing individuals into a space. While the underlying structural drivers of poor representation are often discussed, this focus on the individual is inescapable, whether we are talking about politics, sport, or the legal industry. Considering debates about the representation and status of women, Catherine Rottenberg has located this viewpoint as part of a broader form of what she calls "neoliberal feminism,"[53] a form of feminism that is uncritical of neoliberalism itself and that produces a "neoliberal feminist subject":

> Individuated in the extreme, this subject is feminist in the sense that she is distinctly aware of current inequalities between men and women. This same subject is, however, simultaneously neoliberal, not only because she disavows the social, cultural and economic forces producing this inequality, but also because she accepts full responsibility for her own well-being and self-care, which is increasingly predicated on crafting a felicitous work–family balance based on a cost-benefit calculus. The neoliberal feminist subject is thus mobilized to convert continued gender inequality from a structural problem into an individual affair.[54]

For Rottenberg, this form of feminism (with its focus on representation) permits us to tell a positive story about the state of things without the discomfort of acknowledging the systemic contradictions of our social order that produce the inequality feminism stands in opposition to in the first place. More women in politics, in positions of corporate power, and holding influence in cultural positions are wins not only for those women, but for the system— *our* system—that got them there. A bit like the glow of having a gym membership but rarely if ever using it, it gives a positive sheen without the heavy lifting.

This form of feminism has also been criticized for being detached from the problems that face most of the women in the world most of the time—access to food and water, physical security, and bodily autonomy.[55] This detachment did not just exist at the global level, with a focus on so-called first world problems, but was conspicuous even within the countries where neoliberal feminist books, typified by Cheryl Sandberg's *Lean In*, became multimillion bestsellers. For example, after *Lean In* was published in 2013, child poverty rates in the UK rose for the three years that followed.[56] Four in five UK lone parent families are headed by a mother and almost half of lone parent families lived in relative poverty, according to 2020 data.[57] As the late Dawn Foster put it, "Rather than focusing on getting one or two women through the door at the top and waiting for the wealth to trickle down, it would be cheaper and easier to offer the women cleaning the desks in banks, large companies and parliaments around the world a little more."[58] The underlying logic of the approach that Foster is criticizing is that of "trickle-down feminism" which, echoing the idea of trickle-down economics, states that wealth creation at the top of society (among the already rich) is still good for everyone, even the poor, as the wealth will trickle down the social strata. (Think of a kind of inverse rising tide that lifts all ships.)

The years since the heyday of this kind of neoliberal feminism have, however, seen this logic take a hit. As Charlotte Alter, writing in *TIME* magazine, reflects:

> This version of feminism . . . has been preoccupied with individual achievements, feel-good symbolism, and cultural representation. It has, in turn, paid too little attention to the thorny mechanics of federal courts and state legislative races. Many . . . presumed that reproductive rights were basically secure, and that therefore the remaining obstacles for women were not legal or political but cultural and emotional. Every time a woman won an Oscar, or released a hit album, or got a big promotion, the refrain was the same: representation matters! Of course it matters. Of course it should be cheered. But somewhere along the way, many in the mainstream feminist movement convinced themselves that the soft power of cultural representation seemed as important as the hard power of votes and seats.[59]

Alter notes, correctly, that the flagship anti-feminist policies in the US (such as overturning *Roe v. Wade*) do not have popular support, but the way that the US political system is designed and functions renders this lack of popular support (and widespread popular anger with the decision) something of an irrelevance. Specifically, she highlights the financial and brute political power that these anti-progressive forces had amassed over many years in anticipation of the day when this power could be deployed:

> While online feminists interrogated celebrities about whether they called themselves "feminists" and what "empowered" them most, conservatives were amassing the raw power to pass trigger laws in 13 states . . . While the left tallied the number of women nominated for Oscars and which top-grossing movies passed the Bechdel test, savvy Republican operatives were carefully building a pipeline of conservative judges with immaculate résumés in anticipation of future Supreme Court vacancies.

It would be easy to make this a story of left-wing naivety, something that Alter resists doing (she discusses her own espousing of what she now sees as the "apotheosis of mid-aughts feminist myopia" at some length). Instead, the reality is more subtle and, to be frank, the lesson to be drawn from it and repackaged as advice on political strategy is far messier.

While it is now clear that this array of apparent wins for representation wasn't enough, it doesn't mean that they didn't matter. And at the same time, while it is now perhaps satisfying to mock those who celebrated the wins at the time, it remains true that real-life, actually existing sexism is driving a lot of the backlash against women politicians and feminist causes worldwide. The premature celebration of a certain group of activists does not mean that the real problem (sexists doing sexist things) gets a pass as a result. (This reaction often takes the form of the kind of tedious woke-bashing I discussed above.) As Anne Phillips notes of this backlash:

> It seems to me that nothing is ever done and dusted, that every advance is followed by reversal, and that each generation has to

refight the battles a previous generation might have thought more or less settled. This is clearly the case as regards sensitivity to identity-based marginalization, the importance of which is much contested in an era of "culture wars" and attacks on so-called wokeness.[60]

For those who care about presence, it is not enough to simply secure it once and hope for the best. The work also consists in laying the groundwork for the next generation to be able to fight the next round, when it inevitably comes, more assuredly than ourselves.

The lesson, if there is one, is that representation matters but it is not a panacea. A corporation will always be a corporation and it will look to extract more resources than it has to pay for from its workers, the lowest paid of whom are likely to be women and minorities. Having a woman at the top of it will not change that.[61] In the same way, once somebody becomes a prime minister or president and benefit from the riches and fame associated with these roles, they will, to a greater or lesser extent, think like a prime minister or president who is rich and famous. As I have written elsewhere about such a transition:

> As Commander in Chief, you now exist inside a bubble, escorted by your own private army, members of whom are willing to risk their lives to save the lives of you or your family. The Secret Service decide where you can go, what you can eat, and who can meet. You live in a fully staffed mansion that tourists flock to visit, and occasionally people will jump over the surrounding fence in a bid to get closer to you, often in an attempt to cause you harm. There are around 50 people employed by international news organizations to monitor your every move, reporting their discoveries to millions of people who are also interested in all that you do.[62]

Given what we know about political and corporate socialization (essentially, socialization into powerful roles in most large organizations), the bigger question is at what point we would ever expect somebody, or even a sizeable minority of people, to transform such an institution.[63] It is also a question of what kind of political change we (think we) are looking to bring about. The logic of representation has for many taken on the role of a hammer and, as we all know, if you have a hammer in your hand, everything looks like a nail. In reality, the nails we are identifying as problems might be too big for a hammer. In fact, a hammer might be entirely the wrong tool for these particular jobs.

This section opened with a quotation from somebody criticizing the England soccer team on the basis that it was not representative of the diversity of modern Britain. The eleven players picked to play in a World Cup final sit at the end of an almost unimaginably long chain of prior choices by hundreds and thousands of people. Just 0.01 percent of the UK population make their living as professional sportspeople (this is around 13,000, though it varies from year to year). On average, professional soccer players retire in their thirties, generally between the age of thirty and thirty-five, so for somebody to be a professional, the chances are that they will need to be aged between seventeen and thirty. To be good enough to play professionally, not least to be spotted and signed up in the first place, someone will likely need to have started playing at a young age and then progress through the academy system of a club.[64] Studies have shown that the burden on parents of children at such academies is significant in financial, organizational, and emotional terms, a burden that it is more likely for middle-class families to be able to bear.[65] Soccer in the UK has also been shown to be institutionally racist and globally the sport has been declared sexist on numerous occasions. The eleven women selected to play for England in the 2023 World Cup Final, then, are akin to the finished product leaving the football factory following a twenty- to thirty-year design and build process with innumerable decisions, strokes of luck, and systematic biases conspiring to generate the outcome we witness.

Importantly, it isn't obvious that this process can be fixed simply by having better representation in the team itself. Indeed, to some extent, seeing a more diverse team would be a sign that the process itself has already been changed in a way that has led to that outcome. In this case, the nail is, at root, socioeconomic, gender, and racial inequality at the institutional and societal level. A better diversity of representation in the national soccer team is unlikely to be the most effective hammer.

Political representation, however, can be. It is formal political power that can most immediately and aggressively bring attention and resources to the inequalities that underpin things like a lack of racial diversity within elite sport. I have spent a decent amount of this chapter discussing the limitations of political representation, including the constraints placed on what presence can do by issues of citizen understanding, polarization, and backlash. These limitations are real and they will constrain any politicians that we elect, no matter how diverse they might be. But these limitations are constraining actual, real power, the kind of power that can bring about structural change on a large scale. The fight is a fairer one. This is where representation in politics is of a different register to representation in Hollywood, a multinational bank, or the English soccer team—bringing about change on a societal scale is broadly not possible for these bodies whereas in politics, societal change is sort of the point. In isolation, presence in politics will not be enough—it won't suddenly make it the most useful hammer in every case—but it is a crucial first step. Do we need more diverse political institutions? Yes. But should we put all of our eggs in this one representative basket? Absolutely not. We need to think carefully about what presence can do, and also what it can't, and why.

4

Think About What You Want

All the Way Down

The Front Row Joes numbered at least 1,500—not an army, but not nothing either. Not content with simply casting their vote for Donald Trump, some of the Joes attended tens, even hundreds, of the former president's election rallies during his two campaigns for the office in 2016 and 2019, routinely traveling "to see the president perform," being "among the first few people in line."[1] They were generally not wealthy—certainly not wealthy enough to benefit from Trump's proposed series of tax cuts:[2] as Michael C. Bender writes of the Joes in his account of the 2019 Trump campaign, "several lived paycheck-to-paycheck." This was not in itself that odd; in June 2018, *The Economist* noted that a "complaint often made of Donald Trump's presidency is that many of the voters who delivered him to the Oval Office will suffer from his policies."[3] Akin to supporting a sports team on a road trip or following a band throughout their tour, the Front Row Joes would sleep overnight in their cars and stand in the freezing dawn cold to ensure a plum spot close to Trump's podium. This cost them money; money that they either didn't have or, if they did, would arguably have been better off spending on something else. And yet they came. And they became friends, staying at one another's houses and providing one another with support, many even attending the funeral of another Joe when he died in a car crash. Whatever was going on in this unlikely marriage of a billionaire candidate promising tax cuts to the rich and these devoted followers who lapped it up despite not

How to Think about Politics. Peter Allen, Oxford University Press. © Oxford University Press (2025).
DOI: 10.1093/9780197679395.003.0005

seeming to benefit from his victory in any material way, it is hard to deny that they were getting *something* out of the arrangement.

The Front Row Joes prompt two questions. First, they appeared to endorse something that seems, in a reasonably clear way, to not be good for them. When poor voters push Trump to victory despite him pledging to remove whatever affordable healthcare options they have available to them and cut taxes for the rich (not for them), what are we to make of these choices? They are apparently sincere commitments that complicate the basic assumption that voters would support and vote for political candidates and movements that would give them what they want—and that what they want will be material gains. Second, the Front Row Joes have made their political commitments an outsize part of their lives, certainly compared to the average person. They are dedicating a significant amount of time and resources to politics, traveling far from home and cultivating new and meaningful relationships centered on a political candidate. Is the scale of this commitment right for them and the lives that on reflection, they might want to lead?

These two questions structure this chapter. First, what should you want *out of* politics—what kinds of policies and material benefits? Second, what do you want politics *to be* in your life—how large a role should it play in your daily existence? My sense is that there is a mismatch between how most of us would answer these two questions: many of us want a lot from politics, we want it to give us the things we care about and outcomes that we value.[4] But at the same time, we want to keep it small in our own lives and we don't want it to impinge on the other things we hold dear, such as our friendships or our work. (For what it is worth, if you don't fit this description, you are, statistically speaking, not normal.)

Our answers to the two questions will be linked. Politics is often painted as a sphere in itself, separate from the rest of our lives. But whether we see ourselves as highly politically active or not, when we make the small number of choices that we can about political things these choices are nonetheless very much about who we are as people and what we value in our lives. As such, our political choices should (and will) reflect who we are, and at the same time, who we are is in part constituted by our political choices. Politics goes all the way down. Thinking about these things together makes sense and, if you are looking for a more useful way to think about politics (reading this book suggests that you are), you could do a lot worse than trying to think in a more useful way about yourself—about what you value and what you want.

Imagine that you are a longstanding friend of one of the Front Row Joes. Her choice to focus on attending Trump rallies has had some positive effects on her that you can see—she enjoys the rallies, she has met new friends—but it has also had negative impacts—her son does not approve, testing their relationship, and it is depleting her retirement savings. As a friend, you would not tell her that her activities were definitively right or objectively wrong. Rather, you would want her to think carefully about what kinds of political causes she was backing and how stridently she was backing them. You would want her to reflect on the shape and size of the political commitments—of politics itself—in her life and in doing so know that whether you agreed with her in the end or not, she had at least thought about it. This chapter will help you do the same.

Starting Where We Are

Figuring out an answer to the first question—what we ourselves want out of politics—is difficult, just as it is difficult to understand the political choices of other people. But by looking at the latter, we might begin to get a grasp on the former. Political science can offer some assistance here. Thanks to long-running studies of elections in different countries, we understand an increasing amount about how people express and shift their political allegiances, moving their support from one party to another across electoral cycles. We also have a good sense of how and why these allegiances develop, can be nurtured, and how they can strengthen or decay. Studies of partisan identification and early-life socialization have told us a lot about how our family and friends, our education and work, and the neighborhoods we live in can influence our political attitudes.[5] The places in which we spend our days and the people we spend them with, especially when we are younger, appear to have a big effect on our political views. (Pause for a moment and consider how your parents or grandparents or close friends as a teenager affected your own politics.)

More than this, when it comes to the kinds of political choices that most of us are ever likely to be in a position to make, we are not talking about pressing the proverbial button ourselves. We operate at a remove from the political equivalent of the coalface, essentially paying others to do our bidding in a roundabout way. This is the nature of representative democracy—somebody else gets their hands dirty because a) we pay them and b) they put themselves forward to do so. Although some people are more involved than others, by and large, the actual contact sport aspect of democratic politics is the domain of a reasonably small number of people. A related observation about representative democracy is that it does not seem to respect (or respond to) our preferences a lot of the time. Only very rarely will a policy or initiative that we have some personal investment in come to fruition in the exact way that we want it to. In this sense, representative democracy often has the feel of a meal that fails to satiate you by somehow just missing the spot, no doubt in part owing to the pressures discussed in the previous chapter.

Part of this feeling stems from limits placed on our individual political agency by the way that once they are set in motion, the direction taken by policies will often be stuck to a certain extent. It is in the nature of representative democratic politics that quite a lot of policy issues are simply not on the menu when we are asked to choose what we want. We live our lives in a context that is in some important ways already fixed. Partly this is because politicians, sensibly from their point of view, are mostly keen to avoid proposing courses of action that if taken, would be political suicide. It is uncommon to hear, say, British politicians advocating for the end of the National Health Service (that provides health-care free at the point of need) as we know it, and if you are on either the far left or far right of the ideological spectrum in most advanced democracies, the chances are that your political wishes, such as they are, are unlikely to ever be fulfilled.

Outside of these instances there also exists a bedrock of policies, restrictions, and freedoms that by dint of being born where we are (which we also do not choose) we relinquish any ability to seriously alter. For example, we are not routinely asked to grant our assent to legal precedents from a century ago that we are nonetheless subject to simply by existing in a given country or state right now. If this exercises you, it is safe to say that you are in the minority. Most of us, most of the time, seem, like David Foster Wallace's young fish in water, to accept these background conditions without questioning them too much, if at all. In such policy areas, the default position is already set and changing that is going to take a fair amount of heavy lifting. These policy positions are like a rusty old tap, bonded and difficult to manipulate. In this sense, the outcomes of politics are to no small extent preordained. The deck is stacked in favor of the status quo, with alternatives limited as a result.

Political scientists refer to this phenomenon as "path depen-dency." This has been defined as "a situation where the present policy choice is constrained or shaped by institutional paths that result from choices made in the past." Under these conditions, "the possibility of reforming public policy depends on institutional-ized legacies that structure our perceptions of problems and goals, define the range of appropriate and feasible options, and determine the costs and benefits of policy changes."[6] To put it another way, "a process is path dependent if initial moves in one direction elicit further moves in that same direction."[7] Once one administration starts tackling a policy problem in a certain way—for example, allowing planning decisions as they relate to the construction of new buildings to be controlled at the most local level possible—it becomes difficult for the next administration to do it any other way. A bureaucracy grows around the policy, processes are embedded, and expectations of who gets to control what are normalized. Although other political actors might make noises about reforming this and transforming that, the chances are that they will find the opposition and inertia too much to deal with. Thus, our agency for change is limited—we are on a dual track of path dependency in terms of our own upbringing and early life experiences as well as the political context into which we emerge.

It is an interesting quirk of representative democracy that rather than universally denounce this as unacceptable or undemocratic, we tend to accept it and, in some cases, want the government to take even more agency away from us. There are many areas of public policy where a sizable chunk of the population want less personal responsibility and more government-imposed restrictions that once in place, will probably be difficult to shift. Examples of this include speed limits for motor vehicles, restrictions on the amount of sugar in carbonated drinks, and construction regulations. In reality, most of us are happy to give up control over various aspects of our lives to authorities who we assume know better than we do. I am not, for example, going to be conducting my own safety checks when I board an airplane; I quite reasonably assume that it is better to leave this to someone else who has demonstrated their capacity in this area and gained the relevant credentials. Electoral politics—the kind that plays out in the mainstream media on a daily basis—often consists in debate about issues that exist at the border of what we might think of as a responsibility boundary.

Who Knows Best?

At root this is a question of who we think—and who enough of us can agree—knows what is best for us. In a given domain of life, should all of our choices be left to us or should we hand over control to someone else, usually an authority of some description, who is deemed to be better placed to make these choices on our behalf? The political philosopher Robert Goodin refers to cases like these as instances of "permissible paternalism."[8] Taking the idea that democracies should respect people's individual preferences as his backdrop, Goodin notes how it is "clear from a cursory glance at a whole range of public policies that we do not always and everywhere unequivocally respect people's preferences." At the individual level, we see this play out in familiar cases. For example, many of us have elderly relatives who grant their children power of attorney over their affairs should their own decision-making capacities fail. Equivalently, we also for the most part accept restrictions on our freedom that work against any lack of will we may have to do the thing that is best for us: we wear seat belts in cars so we are not fined and, of course, so that we are less likely to suffer serious harm in the case of a collision. Authorities ban highly addictive drugs from general circulation, making it harder to access something that we might later regret ever going near. Young children are taken out of the care of abusive parents, even if they resist any such removal. As Goodin puts it, "even those most devoted to principles of individual autonomy concede that in certain circumstances it is perfectly proper for others to intervene to protect people from themselves, coercively substituting their judgment of what is good for a person for that person's own."[9]

Even if we wanted to, most of us are not in a position to contest the opinions of credentialled experts on issues such as nutrition, vehicle safety, or construction standards. Part of this is simply a question of resources—I do not have the time to educate myself about these issues to a point where I could plausibly make an oppositional case regarding the substance of what these experts are telling us. For the most part, this system works fine—regulators regulate and the world continues to spin. But there is a more sinister side to this that works around—and through—the little political agency that most of us have. Experts, while often individually acting benevolently and indeed giving us accurate and fair guidance, are generally based in institutions that are powerful and, in turn, are pursuing their own interests in various ways. There will be incentives for institutions to garner attention, profit, or market share. These incentives can lead to actions that distort the information environment in which we exist.

One aspect of this is that authority—in this case the authority of expert knowledge—can be bought. The US remains gripped by an opioid crisis, with millions of Americans addicted to prescription painkillers. A significant chunk of the blame for this crisis has been laid at the door of a company, Purdue Pharma, and a family, the Sacklers. Over a period of almost half a century, the Sacklers, through Purdue and other companies they owned or controlled, cultivated the grounds for the legal distribution of a drug that they knew would prove to be dangerously addictive for millions. Either by paying individuals with the requisite medical titles and qualifications right now or by promising them well-paid jobs in future, Purdue convinced doctors and patients alike that their drug, OxyContin, was not as addictive as other opioids and was thus safe to prescribe at volume. As Patrick Radden Keefe has put it, "[Purdue] funded research and paid doctors to make the case that concerns about opioid addiction were overblown, and that OxyContin could safely treat an ever-wider range of maladies."[10] The Sackler family, despite Purdue eventually being hit with a felony conviction for this behavior, were able to use the institutional cover they had purchased to live a gilded existence as the OxyContin crisis became a full-blown heroin crisis playing out across all fifty states. Radden Keefe again:

> Herion was a street drug, sold out of the back of a car by anonymous Mexicans of uncertain immigration status, whereas OxyContin had been approved by no less an authority than the Food and Drug Administration. The Sacklers were legitimate businesspeople, pillars of American society.[11]

We will also encounter the distortion of the wider public sphere by money, what George Packer has referred to as the "default force in American life."[12] Sometimes this is as simple as the blatant flashing of cash by corporations seeking to block or overturn some unfavorable legislative development undertaken by politicians. In late 2022, Californians were asked to vote on Proposition 22, a ballot initiative that would grant app-based companies an exemption from classifying those workers who serviced users of the app as their employees. Your Uber or Lyft driver or DoorDash delivery person would not, if Proposition 22 passed, be eligible for the benefits that accrued to people classified as employees. Instead, they would, in the eyes of the law, be independent contractors. The ballot took place in the midst of a broad anti-tech backlash across California (and the US as a whole) owing to concerns about the impact of the industry on housing, privacy, and misinformation during the 2020 election campaign. This ill feeling was reflected in early polling that indicated an outcome that the tech companies would not be happy with. They responded by opening their wallets:

> Facing an uphill battle, Uber, Lyft and other gig economy companies set a spending record, pouring more than $200 million into the ballot initiative. They saturated TV and digital ad space. They bombarded gig workers and customers alike with in-app notifications and emails suggesting that drivers wanted to remain independent contractors and that a yes vote would be best for them.[13]

Big Tech won the day and Proposition 22 failed. Although it is hard to say for sure that the amount spent on advertising was the deciding factor, outspending your opposition by 12 to 1 is, I think it is fair to say, likely to have helped. When we think about the scope of our political decision-making, we will also face questions of what we are even choosing from. From what menu do we make our selections and who wrote it? The answer, more often than not, is the highest bidder or the biggest spender. As individuals, even fairly large groups of individuals, this kind of financial dominance renders us relatively powerless. Lee Drutman, in his comprehensive account of the role of corporate lobbying in American political life, details the sheer scale of the operations that these firms are now capable of running, having "achieved a pervasive position that is unprecedented in American political history":

> The most active companies now have upwards of 100 lobbyists representing them who are active on a similar number of different bills in a given session of Congress. They serve as de facto adjunct staff for congressional offices, drafting bills, providing testimony, and generally helping to move legislation forward. They provide policy expertise, helping stretched-too-thin staffers to get up to speed on a wide range of subjects and assisting administrative agencies in writing complex rules. They provide generous funding for think tanks and fill the intellectual environment of Washington with panel discussions and op-eds and subway advertisements. They build large coalitions, mobilize grassroots constituencies, and discredit opponents. They host fundraising events and donate to charities. They hire former congressional staffers and former members of Congress and former agency bureaucrats and former agency heads by the dozens to make sure they have a connection to every person who matters, as well as an insider's understanding on how the process works and how to work the process.[14]

It is not as simple as saying that corporate interests will always get what they want—legislating is a complex process—but as Drutman describes, the influence of business on politics is "pervasive." Part of the difficulty of pinning an exact number on the impact of these activities comes from the increasing complexity of the policies in question. Rather than bringing about wholesale political change, policies in areas including financial regulation, healthcare, and employee rights are more and more specialized. Drutman notes that this specialization plays into the hands of lobbyists who are then able to make themselves available to explain the details of legislation to overworked and baffled politicians and their staffers. In the rare instances that a broadly sweeping piece of legislation does make it across the line, it generally comes in the form of "an incoherent set of compromises necessary to buy the support of a wide range of particular interests."[15] Not only is the content of political outcomes altered; the horizon of potential political change is limited. In terms of what this means for us as individuals making political choices, as Keith Dowding has put it, "if people can rightfully be blamed for the choices they make from the menu of alternatives available to them, they cannot be blamed for the menu itself."[16] It is hard to order a healthy meal in a greasy burger joint.

A more recent invention is social media, which has provided another medium through which we can be bombarded with opinions and information of varying quality. While it now seems laughable to think that the internet could be good for democracy, this was not always such a bizarre notion. One highly cited research paper from 2004 discusses the "democratic potential of online discussion groups," using data from Italy to conclude that "this study supported the internet's potential to revive the public sphere, provided that greater diversity and volume of discussion is present."[17] Now, two decades on, we know that this was not how it went. Rather than bring about a deliberative, considered, public sphere, social media appears to have instead propagated a permanent attention economy dominated by the loudest voices. (In the time since I first drafted this sentence, one of the loudest has now bought a major social media company because he didn't think he and his friends were being heard loudly enough.) In George Saunders's essay "The Braindead Megaphone," he describes a scenario in which a group of people are at a party with a diversity of cool guests from all walks of life. For a while, things proceed as things generally proceed at parties but "then a guy walks in with a megaphone. He's not the smartest person at the party, or the most experienced, or the most articulate. But he's got that megaphone."[18] He starts to speak, telling the other partygoers his ideas about various subjects and, unable to overcome the volume he is speaking at, they listen— "He crowds the other voices out." This has a mounting effect as the evening goes on. Eventually:

> Megaphone Guy will ruin the party. The guests will stop believing in their value as guests, and come to see their main role as reactors-to-the-Guy. They'll stop doing what guests are supposed to do: keep the conversation going per their own interests and concerns. They'll become passive, stop believing in the validity of their own impressions. They may not even notice they've started speaking in his diction, that their thoughts are being limned by his. What's important to him will come to seem important to them.[19]

If we get stuck in a room, physical or virtual, with a Megaphone Guy, we risk losing ownership of our preferences by potentially adopting his in place of our own. But equally, we live in a society—and our society, with its attendant hierarchical structures, throws up its own Megaphone Guys—actually existing Megaphone Guys—in the form of those individuals who are paid to mediate our experience of the political world. That is, politicians, political pundits, and political journalists. Combined, this group shapes and fills the primary arena in which most of us think we are encountering politics. Engaging with this group—the loud group—seems to put a lot of people off. They don't want to be at that party.

All of this is to say that things do not look great. When it comes to establishing why we want what we want, we are running a gauntlet of advertising, misinformation, our own limitations of resources and time, and billionaires' money. Once we are through that, the political outcomes that we are trying to influence are largely indifferent to what we want by dint of institutional design, meaning that we generally, as Mick Jagger sings, can't get no satisfaction. If we were choosing to start anywhere, it probably wouldn't be here. But this is where we are and that is the only place from which we can move ahead.

Becoming Better at Being Ourselves

As individuals, we sit at the intersection of these competing personal, social, and political influences. For most of us, these are neither optional nor necessarily undesirable. It is tempting to think that if only we were a kind of blank slate, sealed in a hermetic chamber and isolated from outside influences, maybe then we could access our *true* preferences, unmediated and untouched by the messiness of the world around us. But this is not who we are. It never will be. Thinking about what we should want from this point of view is not especially helpful when it comes to guiding action (even if it does make for a neat thought experiment that most undergraduates studying politics will encounter).

Philosophers working in the branch of philosophy concerned with how individuals make choices have focused on what they call the "normative rational decision model" as an approximation of the process by which most of us will make decisions in our lives. Loosely speaking, when we are faced with a choice this model sees us—as individual decision-making agents—projecting forward and subjectively imagining what it will be like to be us under each of the outcomes we anticipate. So, for example, if an agent is considering a change of career from, say, academia to professional long-distance running, the agent will project forward in their mind and imagine what they expect it will be like to be them in future, what it will be like to be them on the other side of the decision, whichever choice they make. Will they still be lecturing increasingly bored undergraduates as they near retirement or will their fortieth birthday see them waking at 5 a.m. to hit the trails at high altitude? To flesh out these imagined life paths, agents can draw on a range of testimonial sources. They might read books about life in academia and professional sport. They could watch documentaries and films about the subjects. They would also be well advised to speak to people who have made a similar choice in the past, drawing on their experiences and any lessons they have learned that are relevant.

Even more granularly, our agent could review scientific research into the happiness of people holding different occupations or, in a more general sense, the happiness of those who have made career switches. In some cases, it might even be possible for the agent to approximate the experience of having made a certain choice—in this example, they could take leave from their current academic role and move to Arizona to train with a professional running team for a few months, trying the lifestyle on for size.[20] In short, our agent could collect and process a fairly sizable amount of information about the potential outcomes of their decision that can then be a part of their own decision-making process.

For some, this feels like the obvious approach. Surely it makes sense to listen to experts in various domains where it seems clear what people need? For example, a nutritionist will say that people should eat a specific balance of nutrients and a certain number of calories to extend their healthy lifespans. A doctor will argue that everybody should be getting their ten thousand steps every twenty-four hours. An education expert will say that children are better off playing independently than watching YouTube videos all evening. And so on. We all know this—a quick glance at the bestsellers section in any airport bookstore will confirm that we all want to know what we should be doing to fulfill our potential in some domain of our life, be it finance, sex, or gut health.

But maybe this is missing something. Stacks of unread self-help books piled up around living rooms worldwide (and the apparently infinite dearth of financial literacy, good sex, and thriving gut microbiomes) illustrate that unless we truly endorse the things we are being told to care about, we are unlikely to act on that advice. We don't live the life that the experts envisage because, ultimately, we don't truly want to. There is a reason that the Front Row Joes are standing outside in the cold instead of sitting at home by the fire.

The philosopher Valerie Tiberius writes about how it is ultimately fruitless to try and offer an account of what it would mean for us to live a good life unless that account is one that we ourselves would endorse when we reflected on it. To put it another way, advice about living well and what that might involve can only have a real impact if we actually endorse it from our own point of view.[21] As a consequence, any vision of the good life that is actually going to mean something for us—that will help us as we think about choices we make on a day to day basis—will have to be one that is rooted in the full chaos of our lives, all of the conflicting things we care about, and all of the inadequacies and peculiarities of how we come to want and desire and love the things and people that we do. As Tiberius says:

> The only reasonable way to pursue a good life, whatever its content turns out to be, is to try to lead a life that's good from your point of view. It is possible that living well from your own point of view you will do worse than you would if your life were governed by someone else. But we should certainly hope this is not the case, as it amounts to giving up on living our own lives.[22]

Equally, however, adopting such a position does not give us license to indulge every whim or momentary wish, whether these push us to ignore politics entirely, cast our vote based solely on our own interests, or to post something on social media that we know others will find hurtful. We want to be able to live in a way that will hold up when we sit back and reflect on how things are going. To use the parlance of Daniel Kahneman and Amos Tversky's work on cognition, we want to take account of our fast thinking in a way that holds up when we think more slowly as well.[23]

So far, so good. But where does this leave us in terms of next steps, in terms of what we can actually do to achieve this somewhat lofty goal that combines our immediate wants with our more considered preferences? The answer is a mix of balance and alignment—balance between the things we want in our daily experience and those we value on reflection and alignment between these reflective values and the choices we make throughout our lives. Achieving this requires acknowledging the tension between these forces, accepting the way that life has of pulling us one way and then another and embracing this rather than fighting it. There is a quality of humility in making this move: we accept that we do not know it all and we do not control it all. But it is not hopeless—even if we will never get to some state of perfect reflection, balancing and aligning in a flawless way, we can certainly get better at it. We can become better at it *as ourselves*. By definition, if we take the way we actually live and the people we actually are seriously, we need to start from there, not from some idealized robot of rationality. To begin, we need to know something about ourselves.

Despite the fact that the person you spend the most time with is yourself, knowledge about that person—about you—seems to be surprisingly hard to come by. Some contemplative traditions suggest that this is because you are looking for knowledge about something that does not exist. Whatever we perceive as the self is in fact just passing feelings, thoughts, and desires that take on an illusory appearance of being consistent over time or of being attached to something solid that sits at the center of all of them. Philosophers distinguish two questions here: first, whether we can rely on what we think we know about our own mental states and second, what we know about ourselves over time and how we can come to know this, including whether we are indeed a person with some stable identity across our lives. I am neither keen nor in a position to make judgments on the finer points of these debates.

For our purposes, the kind of self-knowledge I think is relevant is a mix of both—knowledge about who we are and therefore what we want that looks beyond the right here and now. This includes some sense of how I want my life to go in the next year, or five, or ten, what I want to spend my time doing, and who I want to spend it with. This is a roadmap, of sorts, for how I want to live that is rooted in what I think I know about myself.

Quassim Cassam calls this "*substantial* self-knowledge"—"knowledge of your deepest desires, hopes, and fears, knowledge of your character, emotions, abilities, and values, and knowledge of what makes you happy."[24] This knowledge, I would argue, is important for the choices we make about politics. Because, in no small part, how my life goes will be the result of politics—my ability to do the job I want might be affected by economic change. My choice to openly be in a relationship with who I want might be affected by politicians campaigning either for or against LGBT+ rights. In extreme cases, I could be forced to physically relocate owing to military conflicts pursued by political actors. Whom and how I love, what I fear and to what extent, and how I feel most days will be affected by politics. Consequently, when I go to make choices about politics, I want to know, in some sense, what it is I care about across these different domains. Why? Because knowing this makes it more likely that when I reflect on how these choices align with the things I really care about, I will be satisfied that they do.

We can begin to tell which things we really care about and which things we don't by reflecting on how stable our commitment to them is. Stability acts as reinforcement for our belief that the commitments we make are worth having in the first place—we think they are worth having because we remain committed to them. It is a virtuous cycle. Over time, our questions about whether a commitment is worth having simply fade away to some extent as it becomes a part of who we are and what we do, this process underpinned by our initial belief that this is something that is good for us. It attains a kind of authority in our lives. We witness this sort of commitment in the partisan identification that many people have with a political party across their lifetime—somebody might become a Democrat or a Labour voter.[25]

If we end up pursuing long-term, stable commitments that are not truly our own, the results can be personally disastrous. In the final pages of Kazuo Ishiguro's novel, *The Remains of the Day*, the protagonist, Mr Stevens, sitting with a stranger on a bench by the sea, discusses his life and work as a butler. Looking back, Mr Stevens worries that he has not spent his time wisely, that he committed too much of himself to his former employer, Lord Darlington. Insisting that Lord Darlington "wasn't a bad man," Stevens compares himself to Darlington, lamenting that

> at least he had the privilege of being able to say at the end of his life that he had made his own mistakes . . . He chose a certain path in life, it proved to be a misguided one, but there, he chose it, he can say that at least. As for myself, I cannot even claim that. You see, I *trusted*. I trusted in his lordship's wisdom. All those years I served him, I trusted I was doing something worthwhile. I can't even say I made my own mistakes. Really—one has to ask oneself—what dignity is there in that?[26]

Stevens, reflecting on his life, appears to come to the conclusion— or gets close enough to it to provoke some emotional discomfort— that the values he held so dear and that guided his behavior were inappropriate. These values failed to give him a sense of agency and they stripped him of dignity. The values of service and duty that guided Stevens's choices ultimately led him astray. Why is this? Perhaps the clearest answer, certainly in the case of Stevens, is that he did not give over enough time to reflect on what he was doing at various points during his life. (Indeed, it is worth noting that the man Stevens speaks to on the pier bench at the end of the novel ultimately encourages him to stop reflecting now he has started—"Don't keep looking back all the time, you're bound to get depressed.")

At the other end of the spectrum, we often make fleeting commitments that can also be problematic—to people who we probably won't see much of in future, hobbies that require purchasing equipment that is rapidly relegated to a dusty cupboard, to drunken holiday plans that seem less obviously a good idea the following morning. Politically, self-knowledge can help us guard against being caught up in the moment, bending our desires to the will of a charismatic politician who, all else being equal, doesn't want to use power in a way that would align with our values. In some sense, having a good grasp of what we want and what makes things go well for us can help us to avoid the political equivalent of fast food—making choices to support candidates and movements that after the initial sugar rush fades, prove unsatisfying even if they are moreish.[27] Self-knowledge might prompt us to disregard appeals regarding things that we know would not work out well for us or it may prompt us to pause and reflect before moving ahead. The point is that either as an accelerator or a brake, self-knowledge helps us to keep our choices, values, and commitments aligned.

In many cases, though, this process won't run so smoothly and we will see conflict arising between our values as a result of our values regarding both ourselves, other people we care about, and specific political appeals. The crux of politics is disagreements of this kind; without disagreement, there would be no politics. And simply knowing that these conflicts in our values exist doesn't automatically resolve them—we have to face up to them.

When We Think About Politics, We Think About Who We Are

On any given day, I have multiple things that I want to do—I want to write some of my (overdue) book, go for a run, enjoy a longish lunch, watch some television, and drink a cold beer. But I also want to spend time with my partner and I want to eat healthily and cook a meal from scratch. I might also want to read the novel

I am currently getting through, speak to some friends, catch up on quotidian work emails, and clean the bathroom. (I don't even have children, which would only increase the length of this list.) To put it more formally, I have lots of goals and it is simply not possible for me to achieve all of them right now. These goals are in conflict. Sometimes these conflicts will run deeper. For example, a person of religious faith might encounter an event in their life that calls this faith into question, affecting their sense of who they are. Somebody who is the sole breadwinner for their family may conclude that their well-paid job makes them unbearably unhappy but they equally do not want to let their spouse and children down by quitting it and introducing financial precarity into their lives.

Politically, we often hear our leaders tell us that they have to make difficult choices about incompatible goals—for example, slowing the destruction of climate change while continuing to grow the economy, forgiving student debt while balancing the books, and incentivizing the unemployed to find work while not allowing them to starve. (To my mind, most of these goals are far from incompatible and are not even particularly difficult choices, but that is not my focus in the present discussion.) Instead, I want to focus on the rest of us who aren't elected politicians but who still have to evaluate and make political choices.

These choices are less dramatic, for sure, but can still weigh heavily on us. Many of us grow up in families that identify with a political party—a Labour family or a Republican family, for example. As we grow older and develop a political identity that may be different from that of our parents, we might find ourselves wanting to vote for a different political party. You might think this is actually nothing to worry about as we vote via a secret ballot. This is true, but also misses the point. If our father was to ask us who we voted for and we answered honestly, we could reasonably expect him to be upset or disappointed by our answer. Alternatively, if we say that we voted for the "family party," we would be lying to a parent. Neither option is attractive and both speak to the difficulty of making political choices that are authentic to who we are—in this case, being somebody who knows their own mind and wants to use their vote to this end as well as somebody who has a good, honest relationship with their parents, a relationship that we value.

In this domestic domain, the rise of Donald Trump to the US presidency has brought people's conflicting values to the fore in what feels like an unprecedented way, with numerous reports of family members no longer speaking to one another owing to a parent or friend's support for the MAGA candidate or, indeed, for not supporting him at all. The divisiveness of Trump has also tested people's longstanding sense of partisan attachment, with "Never Trumpers" changing the habit of a lifetime to switch their vote from the Republican to the Democratic party.[28] For many of us, such a shift in allegiance would be a wrench. Our voting behavior is shaped heavily by those closest to us, people we presumably care about. In leaving our partisan identity behind, we are leaving a version of ourselves behind too. We know that the conflict between our values leading to a choice like this will run deep. In 2021, *Time* magazine spoke to members of families that had split along lines of support for Trump. One man whose parents supported the then-president said that he had a "moral problem" with their choice:

> Soren, who lives in Los Angeles, finds it incomprehensible that the same parents who taught him the importance of civility, politeness and decency could have supported President Trump. He is mystified as to why they couldn't see the same homophobic and racist behavior and instincts that he saw, and why they didn't recognize that a vote for Trump was a vote against justice.[29]

The clash of values also went the other way. Soren's mother, Mary, said "it was very hurtful that neither of our kids could appreciate our decision to make our own decision based upon the things that we thought were important." The children did not value what the parents valued politically, and vice versa, even though both valued their connection to each other. The conflict between their family values and political values was a deep one and this should not be a surprise—political values affect all domains of our lives. These parents are hurt because this is about who they are—that is, what they value—and their children's—children they value—judgment of that. When we think about politics, we think about who we are.

And it isn't just commitments to a certain party, or candidate, or to others we know and care about that are in play here. The nature of politics is such that we can have commitments to more or less abstract ideas—ideologies—and, generally through these ideas, have commitments to certain values regarding other people that we have never met. For example, we might be committed to notions of justice or equality and, through these, therefore be committed to the redistribution of wealth and resources (including our own) among all the people in our city or country, whether we know them personally or not. For families divided by their feelings about Donald Trump's presidency, it was often how Trump's administration treated other people that these families were unlikely to know at all that ultimately served to push them apart. Some found it "hard to overlook Trump's cuts to the number of refugees, disparagement of women, mishandling of the virus and use of 'alternative facts.'"[30] For others, commitments to various ideological tenets were paramount as people valued the ideal of "small government" or the Second Amendment. The abstract becomes deeply personal in these cases.

Although we might not be in this exact position, we are used to muddling through in situations where we have values that are in conflict. We juggle schedules, tell white lies, avoid certain situations or certain people. And often muddling through is the best we can do—we try to find some compatibility between conflicting values where we can. As Tiberius puts it, "To come to see some of your commitments as harmful in the light of other commitments is not (at least not necessarily) to lose the feelings for the former.

But seeing things in this new light does change the character of our responses."[31] Muddling through, making do, compromising—these options are all the more appealing when the alternative is to jettison one of the values that are in conflict, something that may involve not speaking to a parent or friend or, alternatively, somehow giving up on our political views, potentially recusing ourselves from participation in or discussion of civic life. This would be a high price to pay.

The kind of reflection that we are talking about in this chapter—thinking explicitly about whether we are living in a way that we want to or whether we could live a better life—is not something we do, or would want to do, all the time. Sometimes, even if we want to, we often lack either the time or space for reflection. Sometimes this lack of reflection is forced on us, either in a given moment where there is not time to reflect in the way we would like to or systematically, when we are forced to devote our time and energies elsewhere to sustain ourselves. Indeed, sometimes not reflecting will be appropriate: some activities—playing sports, having sex, enjoying a work of art—require us to be absorbed in them, to not be reflecting or, as Tiberius puts it, "wondering what the point of them is and how they fit into our lives."[32] Where does politics sit on this spectrum? Is it something that requires, even demands, sober and thoughtful reflection or is it something that should be driven by our passions, our absorption in the experience of the moment?

There is a vast body of political science research on the topic of deliberative democracy—a form of democratic political practice that is designed to provide participants with differing perspectives on an issue (from a range of expert and lay sources), give them space to discuss these with their peers, and to come to an informed, reasoned conclusion. Deliberative democracy may be familiar to readers as the underpinning ethos of what have been called "democratic innovations." These have most notably included citizens assemblies on issues from Climate Change to Brexit, participatory budget setting for city councils, and online forums of various kinds.[33] Such innovations provide clear opportunities for reflection, with time, space, and resources dedicated to this activity alone. But these innovations are also, despite their increasing number, rare. The likelihood that anybody reading this has been involved in one of these schemes, certainly the more intense kind, is low.

As such, we need to think about how—and where and when—we might find more quotidian opportunities to reflect. This is not as simple as it sounds. Give or take thirty minutes, the average adult in advanced Western capitalist democracies has about five hours of leisure time a day. This includes consuming media of various sorts, seeing friends, and other activities including exercising or, presumably, doing nothing much at all.[34] Political scientists have referred to this time as "discretionary time"—"the time beyond that necessary to attend to [your] necessary functions."[35] The amount of discretionary time any one person has can vary quite significantly: most, though not all, people need to work to obtain earnings that pay for their food and shelter. Certain jobs provide greater flexibility as regards when and how much and where an employee needs to be to do their work, all things that can affect discretionary time. Equally, if someone is able to live off either inherited wealth or previously accumulated savings, they will not need to work at all. Having children or dependents of various kinds is likely to reduce discretionary time, with caring responsibilities taking precedence (cooking, cleaning, cajoling). Furthermore, some people require more rest than others, so will sleep for longer. People move about the world at different speeds, live in different climates, and have access to different time-saving technologies.

I think we can start by accepting the fact (without necessarily approving of it) that most people are not in a position to suddenly start spending their evenings and/or weekends reflecting on what they *truly* want and how this might relate to their political choices. Instead, it is more fruitful to look at what people already do—consume media, speak to their neighbors, exist in the world—and ask whether there is room to increase the amount of reflection that these activities might prompt or provoke. Or, somewhere between these two options, a third of carving out space in smaller chunks—small islands of reflection in the sea of daily life.

A majority of Britons now use delivery apps to have takeaway food delivered to their homes.[36] This majority includes, to the detriment of my bank balance and waistline, me. I recently had occasion to collect my order directly from my regular Chinese takeaway restaurant rather than have it delivered by a driver. The experience was entirely different to the usual process of delivery—up close, I saw the political economy of the app (in this case, JustEat) play out in the flesh. The frustrated drivers waiting to collect food to bring to customers who were already jumpy, the harried proprietor of the takeaway restaurant, shuttling between the front and back of house, and me, stood there watching the whole thing. At the time, I didn't think too much of this. I simply felt what it was like to be there—busy, rushed, stressful. Somewhat awkward.

But in simply feeling, I was learning all the same. Tiberius writes that "we learn from experience and that often, the right kind of experience is one in which we are absorbed in a way that excludes being reflective."[37] There is political potential in those feelings I had. Once I was home, discussing the experience with my partner and thinking about it in a more explicitly reflective way, the politics of the situation began to take shape. I thought about the urgency of the labor required from all involved, the dominance of technology, how apps beeped censoriously to hector everybody to work faster. I then reflected on the fact that what was once presumably a friendly, almost intimate relationship between the restaurant and customer was now mediated in such a way that those very customers were now never seen, never known by the staff.[38] This visit to the takeaway was political, it told me something about the reality of life for some in my city and it showed me something of what it is like to earn a living through an app. More personally, it caused me to query the basis of my sense of awkwardness while

I stood there watching all of this take place. We should be open to "the intuitions, feelings, and perceptions that draw [our] attention ... without fully engaging [our] rational capacities."[39] We need to be aware that these intuitions, feelings, and perceptions could well be political. If politics is more a part of the flow of our daily lives than we realize, taking the time to reflect on it may seem less daunting.

Seeing Ourselves

Although traveling far from home, spending lots of money, and then standing in the cold waiting to listen to Donald Trump speak doesn't sound like my idea of fun, it is not for me to say that it is objectively a bad or futile thing to do. Maybe the Front Row Joes are simply onto something that I am not. There is no right answer here and my point in what I have written above is not that people shouldn't have voted for Trump or should ditch their families if they fail to agree on political matters (or indeed that they shouldn't). Rather, if I had been given the opportunity to speak to the people involved, I would have urged them to try to locate their values as they related their feelings about Trump in the context of the many other things they care about in their lives and, to quote Tiberius, "recognize all the ways in which our values connect us to each other."[40] The same goes for people who commit themselves to political projects at the expense of intimate relationships or friendships that they also value—I do not doubt that the world, as a whole, has been changed for the better by the dedication of these individuals to their projects, and as such maybe we should just be thankful.[41] At times, it will be right for us to indulge our political pursuits when they come into conflict with the other things we care about. Sometimes they should! At least, it isn't certain that they never should. Either way, we want people to see themselves and what they value in the round.

Reflection, as discussed above, is a key tool for doing this. Another is other people, specifically those people who know us best—our friends and family. Tiberius tells us that "by observing your behavior, other people see things about you more accurately than you can yourself, either because they do not know the rationalizations you have created for your choices and conduct, or they can see through them."[42] We know this to be the case. "She wasn't right for you anyway," we tell our friend after he breaks up with his fiancée six weeks out from their scheduled wedding day. "You will hate that," a friend says when we inform them that we are thinking of changing careers. "That was really out of character," our mother tells us after a heated argument at a family gathering. It is with this light that we should try to illuminate our political choices. On occasion, we can think and reflect and this will be useful. At other times we need to just *feel*. And sometimes we need to get the advice of the people we love.

In time, we will build a picture of ourselves. We will have some sense of what we want in life, which activities we enjoy, which we don't, and who we want to spend our days with. If we were asked about these things by our friends or therapist, we would have an answer. And this is useful! But even when we know what we want, it is unlikely that all of these things will align in a settled way. Our values will be in conflict—we can't have it all. That is how politics works.

5

Think About Possibility

In the Middle of the Storm

Some physicists argue that if we accept certain theories of cosmic inflation—the idea that space is constantly expanding in size—we by implication accept the possible existence of parallel universes that exist across a vast and many-leveled multiverse.[1] A prominent proponent of the multiverse idea, the Swedish physicist Max Tegmark, argues that rather than what we consider to be the universal laws of physics remaining constant across all of the parallel universes, these laws may differ depending on which part of the multiverse a given universe exists within. Think of a flow chart where some parallel universes exist down one path and some down another. We exist down a path containing universes where gravity, for example, functions in a certain way that results in the laws of physics that we are familiar with. But down another path there are a set of parallel universes where it does not. A way of thinking about this arrangement is that the dials controlling the laws of physics have been adjusted. Sometimes the adjustments will be small, sometimes they will be large. But each adjustment alters the physical laws that govern that universe, and the lives of any people—including any version of you or me—within it. As Tegmark puts it, "Many of the regularities we used to view as *fundamental laws*, which by definition hold anywhere and anytime, have turned out to be merely *effective laws*, local bylaws that can vary from place to place."[2] Seen this way, the seemingly inevitable becomes contingent.

How to Think about Politics. Peter Allen, Oxford University Press. © Oxford University Press (2025).
DOI: 10.1093/9780197679395.003.0006

When we encounter a moment of political crisis, it can feel like we are inhabiting something like the political equivalent of the multiverse—in the wake of a war, when a financial crisis looms, as a pandemic creeps around the globe. When these things are happening, a sense of urgency and panic seem to reveal to us the contingency of the laws of the political universe. For a short time, we can access the dials that can alter them. We get to pop the hood and fiddle with an engine that we may not even have realized was there. But an intriguing thought is this: What if, politically speaking, we are permanently in the multiverse? What if we always exist in this zone and the things we feel in a crisis are not the exception but instead the norm?

We all have moments in our personal lives that seem to alter the way we view the world, moments when an apparently stable arrangement that we had become accustomed to rapidly falls apart: we lose a job, a relationship ends. And in a way, these are just as common for the broader communities we live in: a natural disaster hits, a treasured local pub is forced to close. Most of the time these moments are brought about by either a change in circumstances outside of our control or as the result of some choice that we have made ourselves. This isn't a simple binary—most events will fall somewhere in the middle and whatever the event, individual people, be they powerful politicians or regular citizens, can choose to perceive circumstances in certain ways. Even in the middle of the storm, we have some agency to choose the story we tell ourselves about it.

In Tegmark's example, the fine-tuning of physical laws occurs across different parts and levels of the multiverse. The settings are tweaked and a different context emerges for everything that happens in the affected universes. The dials that are adjusted in these cases may include dark-energy density, electron mass, and the dimensions of space and time. By comparison, in politics we generally aren't attempting to manipulate such heady stuff. In almost all cases, we are trying to change things that we know are already within our control and usually in a reasonably modest fashion. We want to raise taxes, expand voting rights, or build a new railway. Often, we are simply trying to make things the way that they were at some point in the past. So not only do the relevant dials actually exist, we already know that we can control them. If we want the laws to be one way, they can be. On this view, we are in most cases already living in a political multiverse and if anybody is setting the dials, it is us. We do this on a daily basis through the stories we tell and the stories we accept about how things are and how they could be. We are the force that moves the dial—but only if we want to be.

For starters, then, one thing to ask when encountering political situations is whether or not what we see is contingent—is it inevitable that some series of events will play out to a given outcome in the way we are told they will, or is this outcome simply one possibility of many; is it something that with sufficient will, our actions can still alter? In politics many of the things we consider as fixed (and are told to consider this way) are not. They are made by our own hand. Not by all of us, equally—some people have more influence and power over which ideas, or versions of ideas, dominate than do others—and their construction does not happen all at once; these things are the product of decades if not centuries of accumulating thought and action. But they are products nonetheless in that they are produced, and all of us are in some way the producers.

Politics regularly pans out in such a way that we end up doing the thing we thought was impossible, often suddenly and unexpectedly. If we want it to, this can tell us something about the fundamentally uncertain state of politics and the underlying possibility this presents. The boundaries are there for us to remove. But this is a view we don't really hear. Instead, even though we think we have some sense of how we could address a persistent political problem, we don't. So, sometimes we are told that something is impossible and it happens anyway; at other times something is framed as inevitable and it doesn't. The question is why?

Change the Dials

You are a good storyteller. You might not realize it, but you have spent your whole life telling stories. Most of the time, you tell them to yourself in the privacy of your own head. Some of these stories are about things that have happened—the day you met your partner, your first day at work, the day a pet died. Others are about things you would like to happen—when you will get a pay rise, when you will run a marathon, what you will have for dinner tonight. Underpinning these stories is another, deeper story that is not just about things you have done in the past or will do in future, but about the kind of person you are—how you react to events, how you treat others, how you treat yourself. This is a story rooted in self-knowledge. On top of this personal narration, you also tell stories about other people and other things. About how these people and things connect. In a patchwork way, you tell yourself stories about society. About why things happen and why they don't. About who deserves what. About what is fair and what isn't. These are, in their way, stories about politics.

Quite a lot of the time these stories exist in fragmented and disparate form, making it hard for us to draw out the links between them. But if we choose or are helped to, we can see these individual micro-stories as components of bigger stories that bring them together in a more or less coherent way. For example, our views about the economy, society, and government are likely to be linked in some way—they come as a set menu. In turn, these views will be underpinned by some assumptions about what other people are fundamentally like; whether they are generally good, bad, or something else. For each of us, these can become akin to a set of personal political coordinates—in more formal terms, they are our ideology. Based on these, if you were to complete a simple online quiz about your political views, you would be given a label indicating that your personal views, along with those of many other people, fitted with a bigger story. The most famous examples of these tend to be words ending in -ism, words like conservatism or socialism or liberalism. These are political ideologies that offer a joined-up story of what people are like, how we should live amongst and alongside one another, and what we should want. They have done this over hundreds of years.

Liberalism, for example, sees the individual as the most valuable unit of society and, as a result, argues that life should be shaped around individual desires as much as possible. Socialism, on the other hand, sees society as a collective, with the needs of this collective coming before those of the individuals within it. These stories are an amalgamation of other, smaller, ones: assumptions about human nature, about whether individuals are rational decision-makers, about what the law should primarily protect. Although it is rare to see textbook versions of these ideologies in the wild, we catch glimpses of them in the passage of daily life. Stories set boundaries, they give probabilities, they assign blame and provide absolution. They begin things and they end things. They can be action-driving and action-justifying or the opposite. Their function, though, is to answer the question that Harold Laswell identified as existing at the heart of all political activity—who should get what, when, when, and how?[3] Or, to frame it another way, who shouldn't?

What we see in these stories is the power that the ideas we encounter have to shape what we think about politics. We all take part in this process of shaping, ingesting, and distributing ideas, normal citizens and our political leaders alike. The difference between normal citizens and political leaders is that for most of us at least, our ability to influence the content of those stories accepted by others is limited, as are our abilities to persuade them to accept the version of the story that we are telling. For political leaders, getting others to buy into your story and make your assessment of events their own is essentially the job. Some of these stories bear very little relationship to what we might think of as "reality"—independently verifiable accounts of events and actions—and we call these conspiracy theories. Most other stories bear a closer resemblance to reality, but it is fair to say that for all complex political events, there will be multiple stories we can tell about them, and at least a few of these stories will be more or less equally plausible.

At any one time it is likely that one of these big stories will win out over the others. Sometimes this victory will be contested, with vocal opposition coming from other parts of the formal political system. But in others it will not: the story will become a kind of common sense. In these cases, the dominant story becomes *the* story, the ground on which the political game now takes place. When this happens the victorious, dominant story is treated by many as the natural consequence of some external reality, as something fixed and inevitable. We hear that there is no alternative. In everyday political life, the dominant story becomes the container in and lens through which all policies are developed, practiced, and assessed. The story becomes the creator, actor, and judge.[4] A strong dominant story offers generally undisputed answers to two fundamental questions. First, what *should* be changed—what is relevant or worthwhile to even think about trying to alter through politics? Second, what *can* be changed—even if we want to change something, what is it possible to actually change? Key political disputes usually run along these lines, either implicitly or explicitly. Should railways be nationalized? Should funding be moved from one area to another? Can we actually nationalize railways? Can we afford to reallocate that funding? The policies that governments pursue will, a few times removed, be in some way a response to these questions.

We see the effects of this dominance most clearly in the fact that policy change can only ever go so far when working within a dominant story. Political scientists have argued that policymaking has three main elements: the broad goals of policymaking in a certain field; the specific policies used to achieve those goals; and the particular way in which those policies function.[5] Most of the time, policy change happens in the second and third categories—tinkering with an existing policy to change who it impacts or introducing a new policy that is predicted to be better at achieving the goals of the policymakers than the existing one. These may appear to be significant changes but in reality the goals themselves remain untouched, beyond the realm of policy change. And this isn't necessarily because people have, either individually or collectively, decided that they want to keep the same goals or that these general methods are the best way to achieve them. Rather it is because the goals, the policies, and the working of the policies all exist within a bigger story that doesn't just define these things but also defines the problem that they are trying to solve. The story doesn't just tell you what to do, it tells you what is and what can be. And it does this without you explicitly realizing that it is happening. You take it for granted.

During the British General Election of 2019 the Labour Party, led by left-wing veteran Jeremy Corbyn, campaigned for votes on the basis of a manifesto that included commitments to increase public spending on the NHS, impose more severe measures to combat climate change, and to undertake a broader program of costly infrastructure building. At the time, these proposals were maligned by many in the media and the Westminster bubble, seen as profligate spending of money that the country did not have. For many, the plan that Labour had put forward was simply not a credible one. Less than four months later, the United Kingdom was in the grip of the COVID-19 pandemic. Citizens were asked to stay in their homes, the number killed by the disease increased each day, and the economy (as measured by things like employment figures, spending in shops, bars and restaurants, and the state of the stock market) was in freefall. The government offered billions of pounds in grants and loans for businesses, a de facto blank cheque for NHS funding, and billions more on wage support for workers facing reduced hours and income. The government, a Conservative government that four months earlier had derided the idea that more money should be spent on such things, had not only caught up to Labour's spending plans but had blown past them. The story had changed.

Breaking from the dominant story in this way is often justified by an appeal to the extraordinary circumstances decision-makers find themselves in—a new situation requires a new story. This is when we hear the familiar refrain that these are not appropriate times for "politicizing" any crisis. Harsh questions can wait for another time. But most of the time this supposed "politicizing" is just asking the fundamental questions made obvious by the crisis, the most obvious of which is if the story has suddenly changed, why were you (and by extension, the rest of us) so wedded to the other one? Political scientists refer to these moments as "critical junctures." They reveal to us the fragile nature of our political settlement and we are understandably curious. They leave us wanting to interrogate the basics. Why is that like this? What is this for? Why do we do this and not that? In many ways, rather than being exceptional states that exist beyond normal politics, these moments instead lay politics bare, showing us its core traits of contingency, uncertainty, and possibility. We learn that political leaders can break the rules and that things that seemed inevitable no longer are. Maybe our leaders genuinely didn't know they could do this, or maybe they chose not to. Either way, we would be forgiven for getting hung up on the same point; once you do know you can change the dials controlling the laws of the universe, why wouldn't you do this more often?

Managing the Inevitable

In PBS' oral history of the 2008 financial crisis, *The Fallout from Lehman*, the economist and former adviser to Barack Obama, Austan Goolsbee, describes the events of that autumn as follows: "By the fall of 2008, Secretary Paulson and the administration are calling then-candidate Obama, and they are saying: 'Look, we think the world is close to coming to an end, and we really need your support. What do you want to do?'"[6] Although presumably para-phrasing the precise words, the thrust of what he is reporting is clear—the sense among these very powerful people was that the *world* was ending. With the exception of a small number of extremely rare events, statements of this kind are generally an exag-geration. Luckily for us, it generally is unlikely that the world itself is actually ending. But like the distress of children who have lost a favorite teddy bear, these statements are the result of a world-view that is either very narrow or, more commonly, quite unstable, reliant on one or two pillars for all of its support. The 2008 finan-cial crisis felt like the world was ending because the world that we and our leaders had ended up living within was propped up by a single story. Over time, we had come to accept that story and its implications to the point that we no longer recognized that it was a story *about* the world and not *actually* the world itself. We had eliminated that gap between what was said and what was. When the foundations failed, was it any wonder that everything around us began to wobble?

The 2008 financial crisis hit us so hard because in terms of com-peting stories about how we should structure our economic life, most of those with the power to make major political decisions had long assumed that the contest was over. There have been two major stories told about the economy in the last century or so. The first, Keynesian demand management, dominated up until the late 1970s. The second, neoliberalism, has dominated ever since. Some broad and brief definitions: Keynesianism grew out of the writings of Scottish economist John Maynard Keynes, principally from his work in the 1930s. Keynes's big idea was that government spending could be used to manage broader economic behavior. This means that according to Keynes, the government could stim-ulate the economy and prompt economic growth by increasing state spending. As the state spent more, more money made its way to individuals across the country who, in turn, spent a greater amount. As demand rose, industry would respond by increasing supply.[7] Neoliberalism takes a different view. For neoliberalism, the general idea is that economic growth is best achieved by the state taking on as small a role in economic affairs as possible. If the government does what Keynes suggested and looks to increase demand through state spending, neoliberals argue that there is a risk of private enterprise being crowded out. For them, the best way to manage levels of supply and demand is to leave this up to the agglomerated decisions of individual economic actors, all acting rationally, in the form of a market.

Immediately following the Second World War and for a few decades after, Keynesianism was the dominant economic approach of successive UK governments, shaping the political projects they pursued. This changed with the election of Margaret Thatcher's Conservative government in 1979 and the UK was witness to a shift in the big story that governed politics—Thatcher, in other words, successfully moved the dials of the political universe. The question of how neoliberalism got to this point, how it won, is complex and contested, but a common view is that its eventual dominance arose out of a crisis that Keynesianism faced in the 1970s. Throughout that decade, its core assumptions appeared to have been dismantled by the events that unfolded, leaving it staggering, just about remaining on its feet. By the time Thatcher entered Downing Street, it didn't take much more than a gentle push to floor it completely.

What we saw in the case of the late 1970s was a story losing its capacity to convince and being replaced by another that seemed to offer a better account of what people were witnessing around them. This shift gave us a chance to identify how each story worked, how each dominated, and how each shaped common understandings of what politics was and what it could do. Like sunlight hitting a painting from a certain angle, the move from Keynesianism to neoliberalism showed us the machinations behind the thing we had previously taken for granted. There is another subplot here, which is that regardless of what one thinks of the substance of the two competing stories, the replacement of one by the other when one appears to fail has an intuitive appeal. It suggests that there is some process of correction and learning going on, of discarding that which is no longer of use and adjusting our assumptions and expectations as we move through time. There is something reassuring about witnessing the passing of the baton. But our ability to make a change happen if it was needed would only be maintained as long as we weren't so taken with the dominant story that we forgot that it remained just that—a story.

Fast-forward to 2007. What has come to be known as the 2008 financial crisis began a year prior in the United States as the subprime mortgage sector collapsed. This story is now familiar to many: banking institutions in the US and around the world had a problem, which was that they couldn't borrow (and then trade) as much as they wanted because the number of actually existing assets they could use as high-quality debt collateral was finite. To get around this, and to take advantage of a massive mortgage market, banks bundled these mortgages together into something called a Mortgage-Backed Security (MBS). An MBS is a grab-bag of different kinds of mortgages in different parts of the country that are being paid by different kinds of homeowners. The idea was that MBSs would be able to act as high-quality collateral: we knew how real estate values behaved and we knew how homeowners behaved in terms of repayment. As such, an MBS was thought to be predictably valuable and could itself become a component part of other financial products.[8] By mixing and matching higher and lower quality mortgages and then bundling these into other financial products, you could turn bad collateral into good at relatively low risk. At least, that was the idea. Over time, an increasing percentage of the mortgages that made up these highly rated MBSs were "subprime," held by people with very little prospect of actually paying what they owed, but the debt quality ratings attached to the MBSs did not change to reflect this. This meant that what was thought to be a safe asset to borrow against was, in fact, the opposite. At the same time, banks were borrowing more and more against smaller and smaller amounts of collateral. If confidence in that collateral was lost, so was confidence in much of the banking system. And nothing good happens when a whole banking system loses confidence in itself.

While a few notable institutions went to the wall (most famously Lehman Brothers and Northern Rock in the UK), many others were bailed out by national governments. These bailouts saw the government of a country guarantee the debt obligations of the banks in an attempt to reintroduce confidence and liquidity into the financial system. Through these bailouts, the cost of what had been an overheated and overexcited banking sector became the problem of the state—of all of us—in both the US and Europe. These events were shocking, which we might think of as strange given that the behavior of these private institutions was in many ways exactly what the system was set up to encourage. The boom years were built on these banks having taken on greater risk in search of greater profit. It was the neoliberal principles, these same ideas that in 1979 had taken over from Keynesianism as the dominant way of thinking about economics, that underpinned the way that the financial sector functioned and had in the end led to this.

When Keynesianism wobbled before hitting the mat in 1979, we saw a break from one story that was seen to have failed and a shift to another. When neoliberalism did the same in 2008, we saw nothing of the sort. Sure, we witnessed a transatlantic dance that saw some divergence in how governments responded to their swelling balance sheets, but we didn't see the failed story move on. Rather than being discarded, neoliberalism seemed to bed in. Unable to free ourselves from it, we were stuck.

Stuck

We all know the feeling of being lost but refusing to accept it. "We are almost there," you say. "It's just around this corner, I think." But you actually don't think that—the reality is that you know, with great certainty, that you have no idea where the pub, or shop, or whatever it is you have now been trying to find for quite some time actually is. You could give up, admit defeat. But something won't let you; it would be *so* embarrassing to do this. It is now in your interests to plough on regardless, to hold out hope for vindication in spite of the inauspicious prospects. Now imagine that instead of looking for a pub you are trying to revive an economy following a global recession that in a spot of bad luck, also appears to be caused by the only prescription you are willing to offer. Why won't you change tack? Reassess? The simple answer here is politics. You can't change because it is not in your interests or in the interests of the people whose fortunes you are bound to. To endorse a change, to move the dials, would be bad politics. Sometimes, even the dominant story being clearly, abundantly wrong is not enough to make it go away.

The aftermath of any major political event will see influential voices participating in a competition. The winner of this competition will, in some way, get to choose how the event will be interpreted by society. How it will be discussed in the media. How it will affect our politics, government policy, people's everyday lives. The aftermath of 2008 witnessed such a competition. Was it a crisis of the private sector? Was it a crisis of the state? As we have seen, the available evidence is clear that the crisis was rooted in what went on in the private sector and, almost universally, was not a crisis originating in the inability of states to make good on their debt obligations. This was not a crisis rooted in public spending. In the UK, there was an initial acceptance that the state would have to play a big role in rescuing the economy, and public spending rose swiftly in the form of a bank bailout. This was a huge outlay, equivalent to around 6 percent of GDP and immediately prompted the question of how best to fund it.

Given the fact that the cause for the outlay was in the private sector, one argument is that it would have made sense to try to recoup the money from the source in the form of tax increases on the banks and corporations who had benefited from the risks they had taken earlier in the decade—risks that had since come back with a vengeance. Alternatively, the government could simply have borrowed more to fund the spending, using its still solid credit rating to obtain relatively favorable rates on the bond markets. Or, in line with the thinking of a neoliberal tradition determined to frame the state as a household that needed to balance the books, state spending could be reduced in other areas to make up for the sudden big-ticket item that was the bailout.

Re-enter our erstwhile warriors, Keynesianism and neoliberalism. A Keynesian response would see government spending increase in an effort to increase demand. Demand would lead to an increase in supply, an increase in jobs, and a return to growth that in turn would lead to an increase in tax receipts in the medium term. A neoliberal response instead wanted the state to get out of the way, even in the midst of the crisis, by adopting a program of austerity so as to reduce government-directed expenditure and reduce the national deficit. George Osborne, the then Chancellor of the Exchequer, stood at the House of Commons despatch box in October 2010 and announced a series of reductions in state spending. This included the loss of almost half a million public sector jobs, a one-fifth cut in government departmental budgets over four years, £7 billion removed from the welfare budget, and an increase in the retirement age.[9] Austerity had won. But how?

The most influential move following the 2008 financial crisis was the one that removed any sense of contingency, any entertaining of alternative possibilities, from discussions about what should happen next. If crises serve to highlight the contingency at the heart of political life, attempts to establish dominant narratives around them seek to do the opposite—they want inevitability, not possibility. Some have pointed out that adopting a firmly neoliberal position on the question of paying for the deficit allowed the incoming Conservative-Liberal Democrat coalition government, first elected in May 2010, to kill two birds with one stone.[10] One bird was economic—a full-throated endorsement of austerity and the economic thinking of which it was a part kept the show that the Conservatives had endorsed since Thatcher firmly on the road. The second was political—the austerity narrative meant that rather than accept that the unprecedented level of public spending and subsequent debt was the result of the failings of the banking sector, the problem could instead be laid at the door of the now-opposition Labour Party. Labour, the line went, had not made hay while the sun shone. They had not done the sensible thing and kept government spending in check while the economy was consistently growing in the early to mid-2000s. These accusations continued even as an increasingly substantial body of evidence agreed that this was a banking crisis that originated in the decisions made by those on Wall Street and the City of London and while most of those same institutions were being rescued with taxpayer money. This fact was not some dark secret that emerged into the light a decade later; it was known from the off.

The dominant story remained, adapting to the new terrain: rather than the national deficits emerging from a large-scale mobilization of the state to, in many ways, imaginatively intervene to secure the future of the banking sector, the deficits became the embodiment of all that was wrong with "big government" and a nanny state. The story took on a moral edge, as it became a tale of "good austerity" and "bad spending."[11] Austerity, then, became the inevitable consequence of the collective largesse of all of us ordinary citizens over the previous decade and a half. The banking crisis receded into the background, no longer a part of the story, let alone the story itself. Having the austerity story dominate meant Labour lost credibility to speak about the economy in general—only the Conservatives were to be trusted. Taken together, this left the Conservatives able to give the impression that they had been forced into making a tough choice that just happened to be in alignment with both their economic preferences and that would benefit their political fortunes. The traditional constituencies of the Conservative party in the business community and among wealthier voters wouldn't pay directly for the crisis. Instead, the state would spend less, a decision that a great many studies have since shown disproportionately affected the standard of living of poorer citizens.[12]

But how did this happen? How was it that the austerity story, long derided by a significant section of economic thinking and, in the case of 2008, evidently not laying the burden of the crisis on those who caused it, nonetheless managed to emerge victorious? Some stories stick around long after their usefulness has worn down. The economist John Quiggin has called these "zombie" ideas, dead but moving, still influencing the world around us.[13] Part of the reason for this is that the prominence and influence of different stories, different sets of ideas, about how politics and the social world works is in many ways unrelated to either their accuracy or any positive effect they have had on that world.[14] And this is because not everyone has the same say in whether a story is true or not. Colin Crouch, in his book *The Strange Non-Death of Neoliberalism*, makes this point starkly:

> Keynesianism's crisis led to its collapse rather than to adjustments being made to it, not because there was something fundamentally wrong with its ideas, but because the classes in whose interests it primarily operated, the manual workers of western industrial society, were in historical decline and losing their social power.[15]

Thinking back to earlier parts of the book, it is the case that some people have a greater ability to get their story across and a greater ability to bring down a story that doesn't serve their interests. In this sense, what kills a story dead is less the story itself dying but rather people saying it is dead. And who says it is dead, and how loudly and often they are able to say it, will matter.[16]

Projections, Predictions, Concerns

A decade after the 2008 crisis, *Financial Times* columnist Martin Wolf took stock—"So what happened after the global financial crisis? Have politicians and policymakers tried to get us back to the past or go into a different future? The answer is clear: it is the former."[17] The rub here is that wherever the future takes us, whatever it ends up looking like, we will in some way have chosen it. Every day we make choices regarding what we think the future will be like—what we should be optimistic about, pessimistic about, what is a threat, what is an opportunity. What we will need and value and what we won't. And as a result of these choices we begin to shape the present in response. If we accept that this relationship between the present and the future exists, it leaves us with two quite monumental decisions to make. The first is what story will we choose to tell about the future? The second is who will we permit to have the biggest role in choosing it?

As in the case of austerity, some voices will be louder than others in the debate at the societal scale and we are already beginning to see certain trends in the way that worries about the future are framed. Of particular note so far is the large amount of interest in so-called existential risks, especially artificial intelligence (AI) in the form of machines that can cognitively outperform humans in every conceivable way. These forward projections, predictions, and concerns are telling. As much as they are about what we actually expect to happen next, the imagined futures that are articulated also act as a kind of mirror in which we can see the present that much more clearly.

A common flavor of some of the projections is that we seem to imagine that the fundamentals of the future of politics and social life will be the same but with things added or taken away—broadly speaking what we have now but with new technology, or without job security, and so on. But it seems more likely that we simply don't know what it will be like and it is far more likely that what lurks within this uncertainty is something that will affect the fundamentals more. It won't be just a tweak or decoration. It is notable that it's rare to see any disruption to notions of hierarchy, value, or something like meritocracy. We can imagine an omniscient and omnipotent intelligence, but we cannot imagine a society of equals. At least not yet. Part of this, perhaps obviously, would seem to relate to who the people doing the loudest prognosticating are and what their position in the status quo is. If you are a Silicon Valley millionaire, possibly a billionaire, maybe it is easier to imagine a superintelligence taking over than it is to imagine being poor. And, given that you have so much to lose, maybe it makes a kind of perverse sense to focus on the threat that would change everything all at once rather than the creeping concern of the problem that you see through the tinted windows of an Uber driving you from your office to your home.

Immediacy seems to matter when we try to imagine the future and tell stories about what it might be like. In the wake of events that are often disturbing, always desperately sad—a terrible murder, an administrative error ruining hundreds of lives, a little boy's body washed up on a beach—headlines declare that "this changes everything." Other news is swept aside in favor of blanket coverage. Politicians and pundits declare that after this, things will change. This is a watershed moment and things are different now and we need to make the future different too. But after this time moves on, the immediacy wanes. Other events clamber back to center stage. Eventually, a year has passed. Two years. You look up and realize that very little, sometimes nothing, has changed.

On December 15, 2012, a gunman entered Sandy Hook Elementary School in Newtown, Connecticut and opened fire. He eventually killed twenty-six people, many of them children. In the days that followed many, including prominent former Republican congressman turned television host Joe Scarborough, said that the Sandy Hook shooting has "changed everything."[18] President Obama gave a tearful address to the American people:

As a country, we have been through this too many times. Whether it's an elementary school in Newtown, or a shopping mall in Oregon, or a temple in Wisconsin, or a movie theater in Aurora, or a street corner in Chicago—these neighborhoods are our neighborhoods, and these children are our children. And we're going to have to come together and take meaningful action to prevent more tragedies like this, regardless of the politics.[19]

Six years later on February 14, 2018, a gunman entered Marjory Stoneman Douglas High School, Parkland, Florida and opened fire. He eventually killed seventeen people, many of them children. In the days and weeks that followed many claimed that Parkland was, at last, the turning point, that "2018 may have been the year that Americans started getting really, genuinely fed up with mass shootings."[20] There were some changes, no doubt, with alterations to so-called red flag and other laws that make it harder for some people to obtain guns. But in January 2019, Floridians elected a Republican governor who was endorsed by the pro-gun National Rifle Association (NRA) ahead of his Democratic rival who was seen as close to the advocacy group formed by survivors of Parkland. Although dependent on the exact figures used to calculate the number, one estimate is that there was a school shooting every 11.8 days in the year that followed the Parkland shooting[21] and another estimate that up to February 2020, an average of three children in the United States died having been shot by a gun every single day since February 14, 2018.[22]

In the same way that circumstances deemed exceptional can prompt a political response that was previously considered impossible, some events that themselves seem almost beyond belief can prompt . . . well, nothing at all.[23] Sometimes the contingency of politics brings out our hidden capacity to do something. At other times it seems to highlight our inability to do anything. Or, more accurately, these moments bring into relief our choices to either do something or to do nothing—to play with possibility, joust with inevitability. I do not use the word "choice" to damn the people involved in decision-making following these events. For many, we can take them at their word that they really felt they couldn't do the thing that needed to be done. But just as these moments cause some to imagine possibilities that previously felt out of reach, for others they can make constraints—political, social, personal—feel that much tighter. Rather than setting imaginations free, they trap them.

There is one problem in particular that we should all be looking to free our thinking about. This is the contention, based on the available evidence, that the consequences of our current trajectory of climate change (an increase in global temperature in excess of 1.5°C) will most definitely change everything. The available evidence is weighty, collated over decades and accepted by an overwhelming majority of scientific and governmental authorities. We have been presented with a situation that requires us to do the thing we thought was impossible, or we die. Die slowly, admittedly, and a long way off, but die nonetheless. If an ongoing global pandemic is the alarm on your mobile phone shrilling ten inches from your head, most of the time, climate change is the car alarm going off two blocks away. The car alarm is louder but it's further away. It bothers us less urgently.

There was a trend in mid-2000s British television that saw a proliferation of trashy programs in which individuals who were overweight would sign up to have their eating behaviors analyzed by "nutritional experts" while we, the viewers, watched as they went on their "weight-loss journey." A hallmark of this style of program was an introductory section that featured the overweight person protesting their ignorance as to how they had reached that state in the first place. Their exculpatory stories rested on their exercise routines, their salads for lunch, their buying of low-fat versions of foods and so on. Their continued weight gain was a mystery to them; they did not know why their problem had not gone away. As each episode progressed, we would be shown footage of them buying kebabs on their way home from work without telling their spouses, of them pouring sugar into tea, and generally succumbing to the "hidden calories" in foods marketed as healthy. Their intermittent efforts at health-conscious eating were exposed as a kite in the hurricane of a lifestyle that was structurally unhealthy and a food industry that refused to be clear about what was actually contained in the foods they were selling. Entering the final act of each episode, the host would present this reality to the individual in question, pulling back and revealing the fact that the story they had told themselves was no longer compatible with reality. They had dealt with the alarm on their phone, kind of—but the car alarm was still sounding.

Is this where we are with climate change? We have been putting our cardboard in separate bins, buying fruit that isn't wrapped in plastic, only taking one transatlantic flight a year. Why hasn't climate change gone away already?! We can see equivalents of the two voices above. One, a sympathetic voice telling you a supportive story. "You're doing enough! You're trying!" Another, a hectoring omniscient voice that follows your every move, constantly pointing out the flaws in your story and telling you a different one. In this second story, you will need to change everything. "Who are you kidding?" it asks incredulously. If you were to speak to a representative sample of politicians, my strong bet is that they will tell you they don't want to be that second voice. Why would they? It is political suicide, by any conventional wisdom, to tell people that they can't do what they used to and their children can't either. Occasionally, someone will say the quiet part out loud—President George H. W. Bush said in 1992 in Rio at the UN Conference on Environment and Development, "the American way of life is not up for negotiation."[24] But for the most part we not only recycle our milk cartons but also recycle and repurpose the comforting story that exempts us from putting our way of life on the negotiating table.

With austerity we were told the story, and the story was accepted, that all of us would need to change our lives significantly to see off the threat of financial collapse (in reality, this was only true of some of us). With the climate crisis, this story is not yet being told despite the underpinning force of reality being significantly stronger than in the case of austerity. As a rule, we are being told to carry on as normal, to tinker around the edges. We are moving the dials as much as we can, no need to worry.

But it is not a major exaggeration to say that even if climate change doesn't represent our impending doom, it is roughly in the same ballpark. Even though this fact seems to be accepted by many of us in some way, life carries on as normal for the most part. For example, climate change continues to play a growing but limited role in the election campaigns of advanced democracies, economic growth remains the central concern of most governments world-wide (the methods of achieving this growth often the same as those that damage the environment), and individual behaviors related to climate change like travelling by airplane and consuming meat and other animal products change only at the margins. The varied and ongoing scientific research in this area has been packaged into vehicles of politics and, consequently, it has become a part of stories about society, humanity, and the planet. These are stories about culpability and responsibility, about the future and past, about our children and their children (and their children's children).

What is the shape of these stories? One story told about climate change is to deny it is happening at all. At its most explicit, this approach has found form in figures like former Brazilian presi-dent, Jair Bolsonaro, who seem to revel in those activities that we know make the problem worse. These almost comically grotesque examples are, however, rare. Outright denial is now the excep-tion and far from the norm. At the time of writing, almost three quarters of Britons accept that the world's climate is changing as a result of human activity, with just a lonely two per cent say-ing that there is no change at all.[25] International opinion polling from 2019 suggests that the UK is not an outlier and that this belief—that human activity is at least partly responsible for climate change—is the majority view in twenty-eight countries in Europe, Asia, North America and South America, and across countries of varying stages of development.[26] Denial, where it still exists, is truly a fringe position.

Instead, the other story, the dominant story that characterizes our approach to climate change, is displacement. Where we find things relating to the problem—responsibility for it, the need to think about it, the need to change—we move these things elsewhere. In doing so, we consistently let ourselves off the hook. We know climate change is happening and we say that we know it is happening but we don't act like we know it is happening. We have individually and collectively fashioned a story that conveniently places us just outside the scope of actual things that need to happen to address climate change and we have wrapped ourselves in it, tightly. In his recent book on the topic, *We Are the Weather*, Jonathan Safran Foer writes:

> I want to care about the planetary crisis. I think of myself, and want to be thought of, as someone who cares . . . But these identities—which I flaunt with exhibitionist conscientiousness and dinner-party Op-Eding—inspire responsibility less than they get me off the hook. They don't reflect truths so much as offer ways to evade them.[27]

It's not that we don't care about climate change or don't believe in it—the available evidence suggests that we do. But this care and belief is only taking us so far in terms of action. As a society and individuals, how are we going about this strategy of displacement and crafting this story that soothes us? What is the story here?

We often see any thinking or decision-making around climate change being ceded to "the science," removing the need for politicians or voters to engage. The thought here is that once a sufficient scientific consensus has been reached, science will tell us what to do next.[28] Of course, this has not turned out to be the case. If we assume that there is a similar level of scientific consensus about the causes and drivers of climate change as there is in a daily weather forecast, it is apparent that neither tell us what to do as a result of their content. If the forecast is for rain, that doesn't give us an injunction to do anything in particular about it: we might bring an umbrella out with us, we might decide to get wet, or we may choose to stay at home. Science informs; it doesn't instruct. Science matters, make no mistake—not because it tells us what to do, but because it outlines the options we have and gives us some sense of what the likely outcomes of choosing one option over another are likely to be.

Similarly, we see an ongoing attempt to split potential actions that might be taken on climate into individual versus collective, with some saying that the former are pointless without the latter. This split is simplistic. It is obvious that collective changes such as a reduction in energy use or shifting over time to renewable or other non–fossil fuel energies will force individual-level changes in any case. Enjoy your cheap flights? If you don't stop taking them of your own volition, you are likely to be forced to by their increasing cost as we shift away from oil. Climate change began to exist on the periphery of government and policy debates in Washington from the middle of the 1960s, often framed as part of the same narrative that encompassed the growing environmental movement. Initial policy responses were highly technical, focused on the potential for some new technology to put the problem out of commission in a clean and rapid way. There is something amusingly—depressingly—familiar about this hope of a silver bullet that requires little thought or effort for anybody other than the scientists directly involved in its design and deployment. This kind of solution works behind the scenes, unseen, and a sign of its success is that most of us don't notice it.[29]

There is also a kind of spatial displacement—an assumption, sometimes an assertion, that climate change is a problem "over there." A consequence of this is that although we accept the science and accept that action needs to be taken, any action always needs to happen just over there, beyond the reach of affecting our lives. Initially, this attitude took form in the belief that climate change was essentially a problem for developing countries. I have distinct memories of being in secondary school in the early 2000s and reading about Bangladesh, a country that lay so far below sea level that it could be submerged if the sea rose only by the height of the classroom door. Alarming as this was, it was also a relief. I had never been to Bangladesh, nor had anyone in my family, and although I did know some people with relatives living there, it all seemed a long way from southeast London. Things have changed since and landmark events like Hurricane Sandy hitting New York City in 2012 have undermined the belief that climate change won't affect Western countries in the devastating way that my school textbooks told me to expect in parts of Asia and Africa. But what Naomi Klein has described as a form of environmental racism persists at the level of daily life, through the politics of advanced democracies, and in the writing of international treaties meant to address climate change. We are we and the other is the other and our lives and our actions and, ultimately, our fates are not to cross. Klein writes, "the whole point of othering is that the other doesn't have the same rights, the same humanity, as those making the distinction. What does this have to do with climate change? Perhaps everything."[30]

Sometimes we will know that we are acting in a displacing way and sometimes we won't. "Moral licensing" is the term psychologists use to describe instances where we do something we see as morally virtuous or positive but later follow this with an action that is equally unvirtuous or negative in some sense.[31] For example, you might follow a "dry" week of no alcohol consumption with a ruinous weekend binge or, having given up your time to volunteer for a local charity, overlook a segment of your income when completing your next tax return. The after-effect of the good act empowers us to stretch the boundary elsewhere. Initial research suggests that climate change-related behaviors are not immune from this phenomenon. Households that successfully participate in schemes to reduce their water use go on to use a proportionally greater amount of electricity than households who did not participate in the scheme.[32] The hope of psychologists is that positive behaviors relating to climate change spill over into others. If you use less water, you might also eat less meat, fly less, drive less. But so far the available evidence suggests that this is not happening. Instead, we are displacing responsibility, bouncing it from credit card to credit card like a balance we do not want to pay. A version of this plays out in the international diplomatic politics of climate change treaties, countries flaunting their good deeds in one area at the same time that they demand leniency in others.

A final form of displacement, perhaps the most tempting of all, is temporal displacement. This involves fatalism on the one hand— it is too late to do anything, the time for action has long since passed—and naivety on the other—let the future deal with the problem. In John Lanchester's 2019 novel, *The Wall*, a version of Britain has been ravaged by "the change," a climate-related event that has ultimately resulted in the young having to do stints of national service as "Defenders" of a wall surrounding the island. The wall exists to protect inhabitants from "the Others," those who were not lucky enough to grab a spot on the relatively secure island. For the narrator, Kavanagh, who bears the burden of responsibility for this situation is clear:

> It's not us, it's them. Everyone knows what the problem is. The diagnosis isn't hard—the diagnosis isn't even controversial. It's guilt: mass guilt, generational guilt. The olds feel they've irretrievably fucked up the world, then allowed us to be born into it. You know what? It's true. That's exactly what they did. They know it, we know it. Everybody knows it.

It is highly possible, perhaps even probable, that we are the olds. Each day that we do not do enough, each day that we kick the can down the road a little further, we do more to ensure that we are. It is not news to us, or at least it shouldn't be, that there is a great risk in assuming that the future in all its guises can take care of contemporary problems. Versions of this thinking have circulated since the 1970s. Following the 1977 election of Jimmy Carter as president, the Charney Report on climate change was commissioned and published. The document, as Dale Jamieson notes, "was the first to fully grasp the logic of the problem: 'A wait-and-see policy may mean waiting until it is too late.'"[33] The fatalism of "it's already too late to act" has more of a barstool feel to its argument and is less common to hear in mainstream circles. But at the same time there is something almost liberating about it, the thought that there's no need to worry. We can just accept it, get on with things and wait for the inevitable. The argument is weak in parts, not least in its assumption that the effects of climate change are binary and it will either happen or not happen with nothing in between. This is not the case. The difference between each tenth of a degree of warming is estimated to be millions of lives. We are in a process of managing, not stopping; of coping, not starting again.[34]

But as with all of the stories we tell ourselves about society, the displacement story is also a story about responsibility: who is responsible for what has already happened? Who will take responsibility for what happens next? And, as is true of a lot of our shared stories, even though the narrative is varied and complex, it often has one clear answer to both of these questions: wherever responsibility lies, it does not lie with us. Our problem of course, is that this isn't going to cut it when it comes to climate change. If this story is the one we grasp, it will remain the case that in order to survive, we will nonetheless have to move the dials and accept that one can genuinely be blameless and yet still obliged to act. If we are to save ourselves, our descendants, and our planet, it seems clear that it is this alternative story we will have to tell and the story we need to win out.

Arguments Are Stories

Already some argue that the story *has* changed. We *have* changed the way we think about economics. We *have* woken up to the realities of what climate change means for our way of living. Both of these are true to a point. There is more discussion of different economic models and climate change is higher on the political agenda. In the pandemic age, maybe we are being forced to become more comfortable with uncertainty? This may well be true. In certain specific ways—booking foreign holidays, securing mortgages, and so on—it is easy to imagine that we will all be a little less confident that what we want to happen will actually happen.

But at the same time our stories persist. In the midst of this great uncertainty, politicians and others in the public sphere nonetheless look to impose rigidity, to make something solid from what is undeniably a situation of great fluidity. What is true of our personal trials and tribulations is also true of politics, of our shared life, our shared challenges. Politics exists permanently at this cliff edge of unpredictability and I understand the temptation to cling to the existing story that helped us make some sense of society, that defined the boundaries of the possible for us. Similarly, I sympathize with a willingness to be taken in by a story about the future that does the same, acting as a safety net thrown forward in time to catch us when we get there. These impulses are natural, but they are also foolish.

We need to look for the story. We must scan for its outlines, trace its foundations, follow its implications. Stories are arguments that the world is, can be, and will be, a certain way. This doesn't mean being cynical about everything anyone says. But it means being aware that ideas matter. Where ideas come from matters. Who espouses them matters. Which ideas are considered sensible and which aren't, matters. And, of course, this applies to the stories you tell yourself as much as those you hear from others. Stories matter—they are powerful, action-guiding, life-shaping. They tell us what is possible and what is inevitable. But if we can look through one, think past it, see around it, we can see that a story is, ultimately, just that. With sufficient will and power, we can begin to tell a different one.

Conclusion
Thinking About Politics in the Polycrisis

Disparate, Overwhelming

Helen Thompson opens her book *Disorder: Hard Times in the 21st Century* by offering a description of the state of the world as 2019 ticked over into 2020. For most, the COVID-19 pandemic remained at this point merely a dot in our peripheral vision, albeit a dot that was actually a large, solid object, hurtling in our direction. She writes that "a sense of democratic fragility was near pervasive in North America and Europe"; "Geopolitically, turbulence appeared writ large"; "Economically, nearly everywhere . . . the prospects for growth were worsening"; and "the world appeared at a turning point" as "for the first time since 2009, annual world oil production fell."[1] Summarizing, Thompson reflects that:

> It was into this extensive turmoil that the Covid-19 emergency arrived. While it had its own extraordinary effect, it also acted as a window on the decade of disruption that preceded it. Over the course of 2020, many of the fault lines that had already done so much to shape the 2010s shuddered again. There is no singular explanation of the disruption. Nonetheless, a good number of its causes were interactive in their effects.

While Thompson never uses the term "polycrisis" in her book, presumably a deliberate choice, this description of the events leading up to the turn of the decade fit the term. For example, Adam Tooze, the main popularizer of the term in the last few years, notes how,

How to Think about Politics. Peter Allen, Oxford University Press. © Oxford University Press (2025).
DOI: 10.1093/9780197679395.003.0007

"in the polycrisis the shocks are disparate, but they interact so that the whole is even more overwhelming than the sum of the parts."[2] This interaction compounds the effects of the various problems emerging from different spheres (economic, ecological, political, to name but three), rendering them akin to tributaries merging into the swell of a river, their force combining. It is this sense of accumulation that characterizes the political moment we currently occupy and, by dint of this, it is the political moment into which this book will first materialize.

Consequently, I want to close the book by explicitly drawing out its relevance to our current moment. So far, this book has considered five fundamental ideas that can help to structure how we think about politics (these are power, knowledge, presence, what we want, and possibility). In this concluding chapter, these ideas are applied to (and drawn out of) the very real political issues presented to us by the so-called polycrisis. I start by outlining what the polycrisis is before discussing different aspects of it in the context of the five ideas. Finally, the concept of the polycrisis itself is scrutinized—how does it itself shape the story we are telling ourselves about the future?

Crisis as Context

Noun: collective term for interlocking and simultaneous crises of an environmental, geopolitical and economic nature.[3]

So goes the *Financial Times*' definition of "polycrisis" in an article proclaiming it to sum up the year (2022) in a single word. Other definitions of polycrisis are roughly the same. Adam Tooze lists simultaneous crises in economics, politics, geopolitics, the environment as characterizing the polycrisis, arguing that it is the "coming together at a single moment of things which, on the face of it, don't have anything to do with each other, but seem to pile onto each other to create a situation in the minds of policymakers, business people, families, individuals."[4] In this sense the polycrisis is all of these things, but also the way it makes us feel. Tooze goes on to say that "If you've been feeling confused and as though everything is impacting on you all at the same time, this is not a personal, private experience . . . This is actually a collective experience."[5] Again, we are in this one together.

The sense that the polycrisis is not just "out there" but is very much "in here," something that is happening to us, is reflected in how it affects our relationship with the outside world. Tooze describes how the polycrisis can leave "one feel[ing] as if one is losing one's sense of reality . . . Things that would once have seemed fanciful are now facts." At the same time, he argues that there is value in naming this feeling: "What the polycrisis concept says is, 'Relax, this is actually the condition of our current moment.' I think that's useful, giving the sense a name. It's therapeutic. 'Here is your fear, here is something that fundamentally distresses you. This is what it might be called.'"[6]

There is some academic debate as to whether "crisis" is the correct term for what Tooze and others have identified. The word "crisis" suggests that something out of the ordinary is taking place. This in turn suggests that whatever it is that is happening is temporally limited—it will, sooner rather than later, be over. A crisis is a crisis because things are unusually bad, but only for a time. The badness will pass. The kinds of things described under the label of the polycrisis possess, however, a greater sense of permanence. Indeed, it is difficult to think beyond these circumstances whether we turn around and cast our minds back in time or whether we project forward to various imagined futures. While some of the personnel involved will change and some of the texture of the problems might vary, the very fact of the presence (the continued presence) of the problems doesn't seem to be in doubt. We fully inhabit the polycrisis, and it fully inhabits us.

As the anthropologists David Henig and Daniel M. Knight have suggested, "There must be a point when crisis-as-context ceases to be a crisis at all and instead becomes a fundamental feature of the system"[7]—this is like the way that some household item needing repair (a broken tap, a defective lightbulb) over time becomes not something that is awaiting the fix, but instead a new part of how we live in that space. This is crisis as context, not as aberration: "chronic crisis," in the words of Henrik Vigh.[8] The work of this chapter does not turn on the intricacies of this debate regarding what constitutes a crisis and what constitutes a "new normal." I would argue, however, that at the level of the individual, it does seem to be the case that the last few years (the time period it is argued is encompassed by the polycrisis) feels different. While admittedly an imprecise measure of the polycrisis taking hold, survey data suggests that even between just 2021 and 2023, Americans' levels of confidence in the future of the country has declined by 8 percent, and the percentage of Americans who think life was better for people like them fifty years ago has increased by 15 percent since 2021.[9] The mood music is not positive.

This sense that the polycrisis is akin to a mental state suggests that it runs deep, affecting our lives in complicated ways. In terms of our outward-facing life, it affects what we see in the world around us, changing how we consume and socialize. When we turn inward, it affects our emotions and our thoughts about the future. The polycrisis runs all the way down to the fundamentals. Of course, the fundamentals are what this book has been about; the fundamental ideas that I have argued structure our interaction with politics in all its forms. As such, these ideas should be able to take us some way to thinking about the polycrisis.

Anybody's Guess

The scale of the problems of the polycrisis can be daunting, making the actions of any one person feel completely inadequate to the task of addressing the issue at hand. The levels of CO2 in the atmosphere (421ppm as I write), the brutal fight for land in Eastern Ukraine, and the role of inflation in driving increases in the price of basic goods all feel far too big for me to be able to do anything about them. This is a question of power, namely that whatever trivial amount of power I have to influence how things go in the world, it doesn't feel like enough to make a noticeable difference to the direction of events like these.

One question we can ask ourselves in these instances is whether or not our action having an effect is the only reason we would take that action? Do we recycle the plastic packaging that our food arrives in only because we think doing so will reduce the negative impacts of climate change or do we do it for other reasons as well?[10] For example, we might be incentivized to recycle more if our local government authorities charge us for garbage collection based on the weight of nonrecyclable refuse. Equally, we might do it because we want to avoid the judgment of our neighbors, friends, or family members who are true believers when it comes to recycling. In other words, although the power we have to proactively address the problem might appear small, there are multiple types of power at work in this situation and we sit at the place where they intersect.

In the section of the book that discussed power, the unauthorized pulling down of the statue of slave trader, Edward Colston, was highlighted. There, activists collectively grabbed power, temporarily, to change some facet of their lived environment. They did this owing to a sense that the traditional, accepted routes of obtaining and exercising power were either unresponsive or compromised in some way by more or less opaque interests. Whatever presence had been achieved was not delivering the goods. This sense, as it turned out, was not wrong. In a similar way, the huge problems that the polycrisis presents us with are amenable to the same course of events, namely a growing frustration on the part of ordinary, relative powerless, citizens that those who *can* actually do something—those who have the power—don't seem to be using it for whatever reason. Representation can feel too slow when what we want is speed.

This frustration has spilled over into so-called direct action protests, usually a form of civil disobedience of some kind. In the UK, this has most notably been under the auspices of a group known as Just Stop Oil, whose members, among other things, lie down in front of traffic, thus blocking roads in major cities, to raise awareness about the climate crisis. To date, Just Stop Oil's protests have been entirely peaceful, but the prospect that these temporary grabs for power become more violent is a real one. The logic behind a turn to violence has been most prominently articulated by the author Andreas Malm in his 2021 book *How to Blow Up a Pipeline*, in which he makes the case in favor of sabotaging key infrastructure relating to the oil industry in protest of that same industry's negative impact on the environment.[11] (Malm argues that while violent in one sense, blowing up the infrastructure of the fossil fuel industry is not the same as violence inflicted by one human directly upon another and, at any rate, that the environmental damage caused by the extraction of oil from the ground is itself an act of violence against the very conditions needed to sustain life on Earth.)

And, of course, it remains the case that the greatest power to cut carbon emissions and thus reduce the negative effects of climate change lies with global political leaders—it lies with what we know as the traditional sources of power. Given that so much of the exercise of power is about getting something you want to happen to actually happen, usually by making someone else do something, when it comes to the polycrisis, it seems likely to me that what we will see in the future is an ongoing battle between these different kinds of power. It will be a story of formal power not moving as quickly as some (perhaps even many) want it to and these people using other kinds of power to try to force it to speed up. It will be protesters versus politicians, visible power versus invisible power, long standing power versus temporary power. Where this brings us to in the end is anybody's guess.

What Knowledge Will Cause Us to Act?

Jonathan Safran Foer writes about the experience of his grandmother who fled her village in Poland to avoid being slaughtered by the approaching Nazi soldiers. It was 1942. Safran Foer tells of how some villagers, including members of his grandmother's immediate family, would not leave. They remained in the village and were murdered as a result: "Those who stayed weren't any less brave, intelligent, resourceful, or afraid of dying. They just didn't believe that what was coming would be so different from what had already come many times. Belief can't be willed into being":

> I sometimes daydream about going from house to house in my grandmother's shtetl, grabbing the faces of those who would stay, and screaming, "You have to do something!" I have this daydream in a house that I *know* consumes multiples of my fair share of energy and I *know* is representative of the kind of voracious lifestyle that I *know* is destroying our planet. I am capable of imagining one of my descendents daydreaming about grabbing my face and screaming, "You have to do something!" But I am incapable of the belief that would move me to do something. So I know nothing.[12]

Thinking about the polycrisis—war, climate change, democratic backsliding—what is the knowledge that will cause us to act? Thanks to the combination of technology and social media, we now see videos of soldiers fighting, of bombs falling, of cities in ruin that we wouldn't have been exposed to in the past. The ubiquity of the camera phone now means that we see what others see more often. The pronouncements of politicians and authorities are not our only, potentially not even our main, source of information on these matters. We might think this is lucky, given the disregard with which most politicians are held—it is unlikely to be something they tell us that gets us to act. Most probably, it will need to be something else, something closer to our daily lives.

Writing about the 2019 Amazon rainforest wildfires, Benjamin Kunkel observed in the *London Review of Books* that "to see the Amazon burn before our screen-bewitched eyes, in grainy digital videos, is to experience the quickening pace of doom as it steps up the pace another notch."[13] This is a statement that feels true—seeing is believing. With every video, every photo, every post, we surely come to believe that little bit more that the problem (climate change in this case) is an urgent one. The screen is a window through which we can look. But windows, while transparent, are also solid. They protect us from what is on the other side of them. As David Wallace-Wells puts it, technology does the work of "instructing us in subtle and not-so-subtle ways to regard the world beyond our phones as less real, less urgent, and less meaningful than the worlds made available to us through those screens, which happen to be worlds protected from climate devastation . . . we find the world of our screens more rewarding, or safer."[14] We might believe what we see, but in what sense? It is different to read stories about what it is like to fight a war than it is to do it. There is a difference between reading about wet bulb temperatures of 35°C and experiencing them. Perhaps it is the case that we will only believe the climate crisis is real in such a way that causes us to act when the footage we watch on our screens is footage that we filmed ourselves.

The Storm Is Here

Another aspect of the polycrisis is a crisis of democratic norms. Some of this relates to the baked-in, structural elements of democratic life, discussed earlier in the book, that can often lead to citizen frustration and disappointment. This is an old story. But a more recent development, perhaps, is the more widespread scale use of these complaints as kindling in an attempt to light a fire beneath some political candidate, grievance, or campaign. A promise to build a wall or stop the boats, to drain the swamp or get Brexit done—the fact that these are complex policy goals that are unlikely to be achieved quickly or in full does not halt the avalanche of pledges, guarantees, and slogans. When those in positions of power and authority do this with abandon but the outcome doesn't materialize (because of course it doesn't), things can become decidedly more dangerous. Supporters are left all dressed up with nowhere to go.

Some politicians do their best to combat this environment while others propagate it. That is to say, politicians talk shit—do not mistake me, this is likely nothing new. But the brazenness with which they do it, and the lack of shame on display when they are called out for it, would suggest that something has changed. Some of the bullshitting is free flowing, a flash flood of lies in the Trumpian and Johnsonian mold. But there is also a subtler, quieter, trickle of bullshit that is just as insidious in terms of degrading public debate. The philosopher Harry Frankfurt notes that unlike an outright lie, bullshit is not in opposition to the truth, nor does it seek to support or propagate truth. Rather, bullshit is rooted in "an indifference to how things really are." The bullshitter "does not care whether the things he says describe reality correctly. He just picks them out, or makes them up, to suit his purpose."

Ashli Babbitt was thirty-five years old on January 6, 2021. Growing up in California, her family were not especially interested in politics. Following high school, she enlisted and served for fourteen years in the US Air Force. She was deployed multiple times, seeing more of the world as she went—Iraq, Afghanistan, Qatar, Kuwait, the United Arab Emirates. After leaving the service she worked at a nuclear plant in Maryland, got a divorce, met someone else, and got married again. She moved back to California with him in tow and took over a pool cleaning business. It was 2018, Donald Trump had been in the White House for over a year. Business was tough for the Babbitts' company and in 2019 a judge ruled against them in a dispute regarding a loan, requiring that they pay back $71,000.

Around this time, the increasingly organized radical right of American politics seems to have entered Babbitt's world. Or, to be more accurate, it had entered her social media feeds. She drank the Kool Aid: Pizzagate, Trump, Q Anon; the whole nine yards. She was on Twitter every day, it seems (her username was @AshCommonSense), soaking it all in. After Trump lost the 2020 presidential election to Joe Biden, she retweeted his posts proclaiming that in fact he had won, as well as those of his boosters and lawyers. In December, Trump instructed his supporters to "Be there!" on January 6, promising that it "will be wild!"[15] Without telling her wider family, Ashli made plans to go to the Capitol on January 6 to "stop the steal." The day before, January 5, she posted, "Nothing will stop us . . . they can try and try and try but the storm is here and it is descending upon DC in less than 24 hours . . . dark to light!"[16]

She never came home from the march. At around 2:45 p.m., she was shot in the shoulder by a Capitol Police officer as she tried to climb through a window leading to Speaker's Lobby. Despite receiving medical care on the scene and at hospital, she died that same day. Reuters describe the shaky camera phone video, taken by another marcher, of the moment the gun was fired:[17]

Videos of the shooting recorded by people at the scene show a woman draped in a Trump flag clambering up a doorway with smashed glass windows in a chaotic confrontation between the Trump-supporting intruders and police in an ornate hallway in the Capitol.

A Capitol Police officer on the other side of the doorway then fires his handgun, and the woman—whose appearance matches that of Babbitt's photos—falls backwards onto the ground, bleeding profusely and visibly in shock. People around her scream and try to tend to her injuries.

Following her death, her brother defended her political views saying, "The issues she was mad about were the things all of us are mad about." Reflecting on her career in the military, he added, "If you feel like you gave the majority of your life to your country and you're not being listened to, that is a hard pill to swallow. That's why she was upset."[18] It is hard not to think that Ashli Babbitt was misled by people who not only should have known better, but who also clearly felt themselves to be able to behave how they wanted, to suit their own purpose, without any fear for the consequences. And in doing so, they led her to believe that their purposes were also her own. When she went to the march, she clearly valued something about Trump and the cause he was espousing. But would she have endorsed these values if she had reflected on them or spoken to her friends and family about what she was doing?

Believing can sometimes be too hard. It can also be too easy. Babbitt had spent the year and a half prior to her death immersed in a world of lies and bullshit, much of it propagated by people in positions of power and influence; people who were unlikely to get shot on January 6. The legal system is struggling to hold Trump to account for his role in the events of that day: as of April 2024, the Supreme Court continues to consider the possibility that he (and all former presidents) should be immune from prosecution for charges relating to actions while they held office. And as I write, opinion polling suggests that Trump, the Republican nominee, has a strong chance of winning the 2024 presidential election outright and of once again becoming the most powerful person on the planet.

"I'm Doing Stuff That I Never Thought I Would Be Doing"

The polycrisis looms large in our lives. Not in the sense that we wake up in the morning thinking of the word "polycrisis," but in the sense that the effects of the polycrisis touch us all. We pay more for the things we need to live a secure and satisfying life (food, shelter, warmth). We go through increasingly unusual weather, dealing with scorching summers, freezing winters, and everything in between. We hear more about politics in the media, in our work-places, and at our dinner tables. It is hard to tune out from its background hum.

For some of us, this will mean that politics takes on a bigger role in our daily life. Indeed, we might embrace this, proactively seek-ing out opportunities to exercise whatever political agency we have. Take the case of the unlikely activists taking part in direct action protests against climate change. One Just Stop Oil activist who had glued herself to the frame of a painting in a gallery in Glasgow said, "I'm doing stuff that I never thought I would be doing in my entire life."[19] The polycrisis will prompt many people to act in ways they previously thought impossible: to attend their first protest, to join a political party, to glue themselves to a painting.[20] For many, it will provoke an urgency, a sense that now is the time for politics to play a bigger role in their lives than it has done to date. It will change what they value.

It also brings home the fact that many of the things we value are in conflict: we enjoy going on holidays in new places, we have fam-ily members who live abroad who we want to see. But we also care about the environment and are deeply concerned about climate change. There is a tension between these things that we value. As was made clear earlier in the book, it is not the case that there is a "right" answer that allows us to neutralize these conflicts with ease. Rather, it should be seen as a positive that we are aware of them at all. Once we can see them, we can think about them. And once we think about them, we can begin to figure out what shape and size we want politics to take in our lives and help others to do the same.

Something We Make

It was February 24, 2022, when Russian forces invaded Ukraine. At the time of writing the war has lasted for over 600 days and, in spite of the unfathomable death and destruction it has brought about, it currently appears to have reached a stalemate of sorts, despite protestations from both sides to the contrary.[21] Either way, with events escalating in the Middle East and with time marching onward, as it is wont to do, minds have turned, perhaps inevitably, to consider what the end game of this conflict might look like. There have been reports in recent months (I am writing at the end of 2023) that Western allies have broached the topic of peace talks between Ukraine and Russia with the Ukrainian leadership, reflecting concern that funding the Ukrainian side was becoming too costly in financial and political terms.[22] These reports were immediately rebutted by Ukrainian president, Volodymyr Zelenskyy, who said that "For us now to sit down with Russia and talk and give it something—this will not happen."[23] On all sides, there is a consideration of what is possible. What kind of future can we imagine? Which futures do we refuse to imagine?

These questions apply to any thinking about the future. And given that as with everything, we have to start where we are, this thinking will have to incorporate an account of what is going on right now. How we perceive that reality will affect how we construct the future and what we think to be possible. It might be tempting to gloss over the various elements of the polycrisis in an effort to create some stable ground on which we can do our thinking about the future. Indeed, this seems to be the approach taken by some of our leaders—by pretending that nothing has changed, that we can get back to a time when we felt we had a better grasp of what was going on, pronouncements about what will happen next can be made with the appearance of certainty. As *Guardian* columnist, Aditya Chakrabortty, describes it,

"The end of history" bred in British politics a lazy assumption that tomorrow would always be just like yesterday: there would be no fights in the backyard, the money men would keep coining it in, and prices were for ever heading south. This rainy archipelago in the North Sea was safe, inviolable and unchanging. The end of the end of history blows away all those premises. Yet our politicians have not changed. They were reared to revere 1990s politicians and to treat Westminster as a gap year before the inevitable podcast-and-boardroom portfolio career. But if they look, the threats to their intellectual models and their careers are lurking right behind them.[24]

Denial is a strategy with a limited shelf life. It is also a waste: a crisis is as good a moment as any to think about what might be possible. Indeed, it is exactly while the crisis is new, a blank canvas awaiting its first mark, that any attempts to define its boundaries will be most relevant. The concept of a polycrisis is itself a story we are telling ourselves (and that I am telling you) about the world. It does all the work that we expect a story to do. As anthropologists Henig and Knight argue, it "packag[es] overwhelming social and environmental processes into a sleek, commercially simple and intensely complex category." If it is a story, we need to be alert to how it is being told because how the story is told will affect what it is accepted to mean in future and, consequently, what political action is seen as appropriate when addressing the problems it identifies. The story matters. As Liam Stanley warns us, "To accept the terms of the narrative is to accept the terms of the solution."[25]

This has already begun with the polycrisis. Henig and Knight discuss how Adam Tooze's conception of the polycrisis does some of this boundary-setting work, work which in turn dictates a certain kind of political response: "Tooze's outlook is somewhat apocalyptic and yet predictable and limited in his offered 'solution'—he cites the need for technological innovation and fixes to combat the 'stressful,' 'precarious' and 'disorienting' years ahead."[26] We might ask whether Tooze is too pessimistic? Who knows. A more interesting question to ask is whether the dominant framing of the idea of the polycrisis works to the benefit of anyone or anything in particular. If we were to think that the current framing is too negative, we might then ask to whose benefit is it that the concept dominates our thinking about the problems that face us?

Asking these questions reveals the contingency of the narrative. It may well prove to be correct—things really were that bad—but it feels possible that there is a more hopeful outcome that we could be talking about instead. As the late David Graeber so neatly put it, "The ultimate hidden truth of the world is that it is something that we make, and could just as easily make differently."[27] However you end up doing it, it is clear that there is, and always will be, a lot of thinking to be done about politics.

EndNotes

Epigraph

1. from *All the Names Given* by Raymond Antrobus © Raymond Antrobus, 2021, published by Picador, reproduced by kind permission of David Higham Associates.

Introduction

1. Edward Docx, "All Hail the Clown: How Boris Johnson Made It by Playing the Fool," *The Guardian*, March 18, 2021, https://www.theguardian.com/news/2021/mar/18/all-hail-the-clown-king-how-boris-johnson-made-it-by-playing-the-fool.
2. Cory Everett, "When Is Everything Going to Get Back to Normal? Taking a Look at the Upcoming Season of 'Mad Men,'" *IndieWire*, March 27, 2012, https://www.indiewire.com/features/general/when-is-everything-going-to-get-back-to-normal-taking-a-look-at-the-upcoming-season-of-mad-men-253001/.
3. Kate Whiting and HyoJin Park, "This Is Why 'Polycrisis' Is a Useful Way of Looking at the World Right Now," *World Economic Forum*, March 7, 2023, https://www.weforum.org/agenda/2023/03/polycrisis-adam-tooze-historian-explains/.
4. Brandon Taylor, "Karl Ove Knausgaard's Haunting New Novel," *The New Yorker*, October 16, 2021, https://www.newyorker.com/books/page-turner/karl-ove-knausgaards-haunting-new-novel.

Chapter 1

1. Matthew Goodwin, Twitter, June 12, 2020, https://twitter.com/GoodwinMJ/status/1271400734614065160?s=20
2. Chloe Chaplain, "Sir Keir Starmer says it was 'wrong' to destroy slave trader statue – but thinks it should have been taken down 'long ago'", June 8 2020, *I*, https://inews.co.uk/news/politics/keir-starmer-edward-colston-statue-bristol-labour-black-lives-matter-440521. Starmer made these comments during a live phone-in show on right-wing radio station LBC, so it is possible that he was attempting to triangulate a view that would please the two imagined audiences of his own political party and the listenership of the radio station.
3. Tristan Cork, "Society of Merchant Venturers Admit It Was 'Inappropriate' to Stop Second Plaque on Colston Statue," June 12, 2020, *Bristol Post*, https://www.bristolpost.co.uk/news/bristol-news/society-merchant-venturers-admit-inappropriate-4222735.
4. Frank O. Bowman III, "British Impeachments (1376–1787) and the Preservation of the American Constitutional Order," *Hastings Constitutional Law Quarterly* 46, no. 4 (2019): 745–792.
5. Peter Bachrach and Morton S. Baratz, "Decisions and Nondecisions: An Analytical Framework," *American Political Science Review* 57, no. 3 (1963): 632–642.

6. David Stuckler, Aaron Reeves, Rachel Loopstra, Marina Karanikolos, and Martin McKee, "Austerity and Health: The Impact in the UK and Europe," *European Journal of Public Health* 27, no. 4 (2017): 18–21; David Walsh, Ruth Dundas, Gerry McCartney, Marcia Gibson, and Rosie Seaman, "Bearing the Burden of Austerity: How Do Changing Mortality Rates in the UK Compare Between Men and Women?," *Journal of Epidemiology and Community Health*, 76, no. 12 (2022), 1027–1033.

7. For an up-to-date figure, readers can consult the World Health Organization's dashboard at https://covid19.who.int/region/euro/country/gb.

8. Robert Joyce, "What Does Yesterday's News Mean for Living Standards?," presentation (London: Institute for Fiscal Studies, 2011), https://ifs.org.uk/publications/what-does-yesterdays-news-mean-living-standards.

9. Judith Evans, "Over-65s Account for Almost Half of UK Housing Wealth," *Financial Times*, December 27, 2019, https://www.ft.com/content/b3847f7c-25ab-11ea-9305-4234e74b0ef3.

10. Child Poverty Action Group, "Child Poverty Facts and Figures," *CPAG*, https://cpag.org.uk/child-poverty/child-poverty-facts-and-figures (accessed August 19, 2024).

11. Inequality.org, "Income Inequality in the United States," *Inequality.org*, https://inequality.org/facts/income-inequality/ (accessed August 19, 2024).

12. Rupert Neate, "Jeff Bezos, the World's Richest Man, Added £10bn to His Fortune in Just One Day," *The Guardian*, July 21, 2020, https://www.theguardian.com/technology/2020/jul/21/jeff-bezos-the-worlds-richest-man-added-10bn-to-his-fortune-in-just-one-day.

13. Jeena O' Neill, "Household Income Inequality, UK: Financial Year Ending 2019," *Office for National Statistics*, March 5, 2020, https://www.ons.gov.uk/peoplepopulationandcommunity/personalandhouseholdfinances/incomeandwealth/bulletins/householdincomeinequalityfinancial/financialyearending2019.

14. US Bureau of Labor Statistics, "Median Usual Weekly Earnings of Full-Time Wage and Salary Workers By Age, Race, Hispanic or Latino Ethnicity, and Sex, Third Quarter 2023 Averages, Not Seasonally Adjusted," October 18, 2023, https://www.bls.gov/news.release/wkyeng.t03.htm.

15. Cabinet Office, *Race Disparity Audit*, March 2018, https://assets.publishing.service.gov.uk/government/uploads/system/uploads/attachment_data/file/686071/Revised_RDA_report_March_2018.pdf.

16. Ibid.

17. National Institutes for Health, "Life Expectancy in the U.S. Increased Between 2000 and 2019, But Widespread Gaps Among Racial and Ethnic Groups Exist," June 16, 2022, https://www.nih.gov/news-events/news-releases/life-expectancy-us-increased-between-2000-2019-widespread-gaps-among-racial-ethnic-groups-exist.

18. Pierre Bourdieu, *Distinction: A Social Critique of the Judgment of Taste* (Oxford: Routledge, 2010).

19. The critic Christian Lorentzson wrote in the *London Review of Books* that: "Reading *Normal People* sometimes feels like doing maths problems, since Marianne and Connell seem less like people than a quivering set of power dynamics. At school, she's richer than him, but he's more popular. Their relative popularity switches when they go to university, where wealth is more salient than amiability. He's taller than her new boyfriend, but the new boyfriend is loaded: who would intimidate whom?" Christian Lorentzson, "I Couldn't Live Normally," *London Review of Books*, 43, no. 18, https://www.lrb.co.uk/the-paper/v43/n18/christian-lorentzen/i-couldn-t-live-normally.

20. Sally Rooney, *Normal People* (London: Faber & Faber, 2018), 68.
21. Sam Friedman and Daniel Laurison, *The Class Ceiling: Why it Pays to be Privileged* (Bristol: Policy Press), 199.
22. Zadie Smith, *NW* (Penguin: London, 2011), 239. Depressingly, something like this fictional event took place in reality while I was writing this book: Owen Bowcott, "Investigation Launched After Black Barrister Mistaken for Defendant Three Times in a Day," *The Guardian*, September 24, 2020, https://www.theguardian.com/law/2020/sep/24/investigation-launched-after-black-barrister-mistaken-for-defendant-three-times-in-a-day.
23. Zadie Smith, *NW*, 125.
24. Joseph Hudson, "What Is 'Estuary English'?," Pronunciation Studio, October 12, 2016, https://pronunciationstudio.com/estuary-english/.
25. David Rosewarne, "Estuary English: Tomorrow's RP?," *English Today* 10, no. 1 (1994): 3–8, at 8.
26. Friedman and Laurison, *The Class Ceiling*, 128.
27. J. P. Jamieson, "The Home Field Advantage in Athletics: A Meta-Analysis," *Journal of Applied Social Psychology*, 40, no. 7 (2010): 1819–1848.; Mark S. Allen and Marc V. Jones, "The Home Advantage Over the First 20 Seasons of the English Premier League: Effects of Shirt Colour, Team Ability and Time Trends," *International Journal of Sport and Exercise Psychology* 12, no. 1 (2014): 1819–1848.
28. Karl Ove Knausgaard, *My Struggle Book 6* (New York: Farrar, Strauss and Giroux, 2018), 331–2.
29. Douglas Murray, *The Madness of Crowds* (London: Bloomsbury, 2019).
30. Murray, *The Madness of Crowds*, 7.
31. David Foster Wallace, *This is Water: Some Thoughts, Delivered on a Significant Occasion, about Living a Compassionate Life* (New York: Little Brown, 2009).
32. Colin Hay, *Political Analysis: A Critical Introduction* (Basingstoke: Palgrave MacMillan, 2002), 186.
33. While far from all politicians are rich, or are from rich backgrounds, even those who are from, say, backgrounds where their family were dependent on welfare in their early life are the ones who "got out," something that often features in the way that they present themselves to the public. For example, the prominent UK Labour Party politician, Wes Streeting, published a memoir in 2023, which his publishers described in the following way: "Wes Streeting might have ended up in prison rather than in parliament . . . Brought up on a Stepney council estate, the young Streeting saw his teenage parents struggle to provide for him . . . This honest, uplifting, affectionate memoir is a tribute to the love and support which set him on his way out of poverty." Hachette UK, "One Boy, Two Bills and a Fry Up," https://www.hachette.co.uk/titles/wes-streeting/one-boy-two-bills-and-a-fry-up/9781399710107/.
34. Sarah Marie Hall, "A Very Personal Crisis: Family Fragilities and Everyday Conjunctures within Lived Experiences of Austerity," *Transactions of the Institute of British Geographers* 44, no. 3 (2019): 485.
35. Jennifer Jacquet, *Is Shame Necessary?* (London: Allen Lane, 2015), 12.
36. Jacquet, *Is Shame Necessary?*, 11.
37. It is notable that Boris Johnson, he who could not be shamed, was elevated to high office not long after Osborne left it.

Chapter 2

1. Gordon Taylor, Twitter, February 2, 2017, https://twitter.com/gordytaylor58/status/827114952523730944.

2. J. K. Rowling, Twitter, January 28, 2017, https://twitter.com/jk_rowling/status/ 825449564777934849?lang=en.
3. Adam McDonnell, "Does Britain Understand Brexit?," YouGov, January 11, 2019, https://yougov.co.uk/politics/articles/22289-does-britain-understand-brexit?redirect_from=%2Ftopics%2Fpolitics%2Farticles-reports%2F2019%2F01%2F11%2Fdoes-britain-understand-brexit.
4. John R. Hibbing and Elizabeth Theiss-Morse, *Stealth Democracy: Americans' Beliefs About How Government Should Work* (Cambridge: Cambridge University Press, 2002).
5. Duncan Pritchard, *What is This Thing Called Knowledge*, 4th ed. (London: Routledge, 2018), 3.
6. Joshua Habgood-Coote, "Knowledge-How, Abilities, and Questions," *Australasian Journal of Philosophy* 97, no. 1 (2019): 86–104.
7. Jason Brennan, *Against Democracy* (Princeton, NJ: Princeton University Press, 2016), 24.
8. Ilya Somin, *Democracy and Political Ignorance* (Stanford, CA: Stanford University Press, 2013), 17.
9. Michael X. Delli Carpini and Scott Keeter, "Measuring Political Knowledge: Putting First Things First," *American Journal of Political Science* 37, no. 4 (1993): 1179–1206, at 1195.
10. Somin, *Democracy and Political Ignorance*, 22.
11. Peter Allen and David S. Moon, "'Huge Fan of the Drama': Politics as an Object of Fandom," *Convergence* 29, no. 6 (2023), https://doi.org/10.1177/ 13548565231203979.
12. Matt Chorley, Twitter, January 4, 2021, https://twitter.com/MattChorley/status/ 1346050621280038913.
13. Winston Churchill, "Their Finest Hour", *International Churchill Society*, https:// winstonchurchill.org/resources/speeches/1940-the-finest-hour/their-finest-hour/.
14. Indeed, the discussion of the opinion polling that Chorley hosted on his radio show took place between a communications professional, a former Director of Communications at 10 Downing Street, and a "lobby hack." Matt Chorley, Twitter, January 4, 2021, https://twitter.com/MattChorley/status/1346105807021207552.
15. Delli Carpini and Keeter, "Measuring Political Knowledge."
16. Zan Strabac and Toril Aalberg, "Measuring Political Knowledge in Telephone and Web Surveys: A Cross-National Comparison," *Social Science Computer Review* 29, no. 2 (2011): 175–192; Kathleen Dolan, "Do Women and Men Know Different Things? Measuring Gender Differences in Political Knowledge," *Journal of Politics* 73, no. 1 (2011): 97–107; The British Election Study, https://www. britishelectionstudy.com/ (accessed September 18, 2024).
17. I haven't done this, but I did (as a teenager) apply for the then-vacant Leeds United manager's job based on a CV listing solely experience gained from the computer game *Championship Manager*. Reader, I did not get the job. Soccer's loss was political science's gain.
18. Kathleen Beckers, Stefaan Walgrave, Hanna V. Wolf, Kenza Lamot, and Peter Van Aelst, "Right-Wing Bias in Journalists' Perceptions of Public Opinion," *Journalism Practice* 15, no. 2 (2021): 1–16.
19. Tony Blair, *A Journey*, (London: Hutchinson, 2010), 70.
20. Bryan Caplan, *The Myth of the Rational Voter* (Princeton, NJ: Princeton University Press, 2007).
21. Brennan, *Against Democracy*, 228.
22. Scott Althaus, *Collective Preferences in Democratic Politics: Opinion Surveys and the Will of the People* (Cambridge: Cambridge University Press, 2003).
23. Althaus, *Collective Preferences in Democratic Politics*, 16.

24. Althaus, *Collective Preferences in Democratic Politics*, 15.
25. Mary-Kate Lizotte and Andrew H. Sidman, "Explaining the Gender Gap in Political Knowledge," *Politics & Gender* 5, no. 2 (2009): 127–151.
26. Harold D. Lasswell, *Politics: Who Gets What, When, How* (Royal Oak, MI: Pickle Partners Publishing, 1936).
27. Andrew Gamble, *Politics: Why It Matters* (Cambridge: Polity Press, 2019), 12.
28. There are others, notably the French philosopher Jacques Rancière, who take a completely different view to this one, but ultimately would probably agree with my overall argument that these dominant measures of political knowledge do not measure actually political knowledge. Rancière distinguishes, broadly speaking, between politics (*la politique*) which is the irreducible sphere in which humanity is able to express true equality and the police order (*la police*), which is what most people, including the dominant measures of political knowledge, talk about when they talk about politics. For Rancière, *police* comprises political institutions, the judiciary, and the bureaucracy. For further discussion on these ideas I recommend Samuel A. Chambers, "Jacques Rancière and the Problem of Pure Politics," *European Journal of Political Theory* 10, no. 3 (2011): 303–326.
29. Delli Carpini and Keeter, "Measuring Political Knowledge," 10.
30. Indeed, when politicians are thrown some sort of test of this kind, usually on a live broadcast, they tend to perform badly. This, however, never seriously brings into question their credentials for the job.
31. Charles Moore, "Boris Succeeded Where Others Failed Because He Accepted the Logic of Brexit," *The Daily Telegraph*, December 25, 2020, https://www.telegraph.co.uk/news/2020/12/25/boris-succeeded-others-failed-accepted-logic-brexit/.
32. John Rentoul, "Boris Johnson Is Back with a Video Message of Subtle Political Skill," *The Independent*, April 12, 2020, https://www.independent.co.uk/voices/boris-johnson-coronavirus-hospital-discharge-video-twitter-a9461771.html.
33. Daniel James, "Why Our Politicians Love Robert Caro," *New Statesman*, May 25, 2012, https://www.newstatesman.com/blogs/cultural-capital/2012/05/why-our-politicians-love-robert-caro.
34. Laura Montanaro, "The Democratic Legitimacy of Self-Appointed Representatives," *Journal of Politics* 74, no. 4 (2012): 1094–1107.
35. Glen O'Hara, "Keir Starmer Is the Labour Party in Human Form," *GQ*, June 10, 2020, https://www.gq-magazine.co.uk/politics/article/keir-starmer-labour-leader.
36. Grenfell Action Group, "KCTMO—Playing with Fire!," November 20, 2016, https://assets.grenfelltowerinquiry.org.uk/TMO00835660_GAG%20blog%20post%20-%20KCTMO%20Playing%20with%20fire.pdf.
37. Miranda Fricker, *Epistemic Injustice: Power and the Ethics of Knowing* (Oxford: Oxford University Press, 2007), 1.
38. Fricker, *Epistemic Injustice*, 13–14.
39. Miranda Bryant, "BBC's Alex Scott 'Proud' of Working Class Accent After Peer's Elocution Jibe," *The Guardian*, July 31, 2021, https://www.theguardian.com/inequality/2021/jul/31/bbc-alex-scott-proud-working-class-accent-digby-jones-elocution.
40. Fricker, *Epistemic Injustice*, 1.
41. Fricker, *Epistemic Injustice*, 147.
42. Christine Bratu and Hilkje Haenel, "Varieties of Hermeneutical Injustice: A Blueprint," *Moral Philosophy and Politics* 8, no. 2 (2021): 331–350.
43. Fricker, *Epistemic Injustice*, 148.
44. Fricker, *Epistemic Injustice*, 16.
45. Kira Sanbonmatsu, "Gender-Related Political Knowledge and the Descriptive Representation of Women," *Political Behavior* 25, no. 4 (2003): 367–388.

46. Kathleen Dolan, "Do Women and Men Know Different Things? Measuring Gender Differences in Political Knowledge," *Journal of Politics* 73, no. 1 (2011): 97–107.

47. Young Mie Kim, "Issue Publics in the New Information Environment: Selectivity, Domain Specificity, and Extremity," *Communication Research* 36, no. 2 (2009): 254–284.

48. Jason Barabas, Jennifer Jerit, William Pollock, and Carlisle Rainey, "The Question(s) of Political Knowledge," *American Political Science Review* 108, no. 4 (2014): 840–855.

49. Cathy J. Cohen and Matthew D. Luttig, "Reconceptualizing Political Knowledge: Race, Ethnicity, and Carceral Violence," *Perspectives on Politics* 18, no. 3 (2020): 805–818.

50. The victims of this violence were Eric Garner, Michael Brown, Marissa Alexander, CeCe McDonald, John Crawford III, and Renisha McBride.

51. Kathleen Dolan and Michael A. Hansen, "The Variable Nature of the Gender Gap in Political Knowledge," *Journal of Women, Politics & Policy* 41, no. 2 (2020): 127–143.

52. Dietlind Stolle and Elisabeth Gidengil, "What Do Women Really Know? A Gendered Analysis of Varieties of Political Knowledge," *Perspectives on Politics* 8, no. 1 (2010): 93–109.

53. Katherine Cramer and Benjamin Toff, "The Fact of Experience: Rethinking Political Knowledge and Civic Competence," *Perspectives on Politics* 15, no. 3 (2017): 754–770.

Chapter 3

1. Ryan Grim and Briahna Gray, "Podcast Special: Alexandria Ocasio-Cortez on Her First Weeks in Washington," *The Intercept*, January 28, 2019, https://theintercept.com/2019/01/28/alexandria-ocasio-cortez-podcast/.

2. Center for American Women and Politics, "The Gender Gap: Voting Choices in Presidential Elections," Center for American Women and Politics (CAWP), Eagleton Institute of Politics, Rutgers University (2017), https://cawp.rutgers.edu/sites/default/files/resources/ggpresvote.pdf

3. Ana Catalano Weeks and Peter Allen, "Backlash Against 'Identity Politics': Far Right Success and Mainstream Party Attention to Identity Groups," *Politics, Groups, and Identities* 11, no. 5 (2023): 935–953.

4. As the political theorist, Andrew Rehfeld puts it, "Democracy is the only form of government that allows people to rule themselves. Ironically, political representation enables modern democracies to exclude virtually everyone from the institutions that govern them." Andrew Rehfeld, *The Concept of Constituency* (Oxford: Oxford University Press, 2005), xi.

5. For more on this idea, readers can consult my first book, *The Political Class* (Oxford: Oxford University Press, 2018).

6. Mary K. Nugent and Mona Lena Krook, "All-Women Shortlists: Myths and Realities," *Parliamentary Affairs* 69, no. 1 (2016): 115–135.

7. UN Women, "Facts and Figures: Women's Leadership and Political Participation," *UN Women* (2023), https://www.unwomen.org/en/what-we-do/leadership-and-political-participation/facts-and-figures.

8. European Institute of Gender Equality, "Numbers of Note: Women in Decision-Making Positions," *EIGE*, April 5, 2023, https://eige.europa.eu/newsroom/news/numbers-note-women-decision-making-positions?language_content_entity=en.

9. Elise Uberoi and Helena Carthew, "Ethnic Diversity in Politics and Public Life," *House of Commons Library*, October 2, 2023, https://commonslibrary.parliament. uk/research-briefings/sn01156/.
10. Katherine Schaeffer, "U.S. Congress Continues to Grow in Racial, Ethnic Diversity," *Pew Research Center*, January 9, 2023, https://www.pewresearch.org/short-reads/2023/01/09/u-s-congress-continues-to-grow-in-racial-ethnic-diversity/.
11. Andrew Reynolds, "The UK's Parliament Is Still the Gayest in the World After 2019 Election," *Pink News*, December 13, 2019, https://www.thepinknews.com/ 2019/12/13/uk-gay-parliament-world-2019-general-election-snp-conservatives-labour-lgbt/;   https://www.pewresearch.org/short-reads/2023/01/11/118th-congress-breaks-record-for-lesbian-gay-and-bisexual-representation/.
12. Melanie M. Hughes, "Diversity in National Legislatures Around the World," *Sociology Compass* 7, no. 1 (2013): 23–33.
13. Matthew Hayes and Matthew V. Hibbing, "The Symbolic Benefits of Descriptive and Substantive Representation," *Political Behavior* 39 (2017): 31–50.
14. Jane Mansbridge, "Should Blacks Represent Blacks and Women Represent Women? A Contingent 'Yes,'" *Journal of Politics* 61, no. 3 (1999): 628–657.
15. Katelyn Stauffer, "Public Perceptions of Women's Inclusion and Feelings of Political Efficacy," *American Political Science Review* 115, no. 4 (2021): 1226–1241.
16. Zohana Hessami and Mariana Lopes da Fonseca, "Female Political Representation and Substantive Effects on Policies: A Literature Review," *European Journal of Political Economy* 63 (2020): 101896, https://doi.org/10.1016/j.ejpoleco.2020. 101896.
17. For a summary see Ana Catalano Weeks, *Making Gender Salient: From Gender Quota Laws to Policy* (Cambridge: Cambridge University Press, 2022).
18. Crucially, it should never be the case that being different is a condition for these groups' presence in political institutions—such a condition of novelty was never placed on the men who previously dominated them.
19. Karen Celis and Sarah Childs, "Conservatism and Women's Political Representation," *Politics & Gender* 14, no. 1 (2018): 5–26.
20. Christine Tamir, "The Growing Diversity of Black America," *Pew Research Center*, March 25, 2021, https://www.pewresearch.org/social-trends/2021/03/25/the-growing-diversity-of-black-america/.
21. Jane Mansbridge, "Should Workers Represent Workers?," *Swiss Political Science Review* 21, no. 2 (2015): 261–270, at 261.
22. For discussion see Suzanne Dovi, *The Good Representative* (Malden, MA: Blackwell, 2007).
23. Peter Allen, "Experience, Knowledge, and Political Representation," *Politics & Gender* 18, no. 4 (2022): 1112–1140.
24. Linda McDowell, Sundari Anitha, and Ruth Pearson, "Striking Narratives: Class, Gender and Ethnicity in the 'Great Grunwick Strike', London, UK, 1976–1978," *Women's History Review* 23, no. 4 (2014): 595–619.
25. Michael C. Dawson and Lawrence D. Bobo, "One Year Later and the Myth of a Post-Racial Society," *Du Bois Review: Social Science Research on Race* 6, no. 2 (2009): 247–249.
26. Associated Press-NORC Center for Public Affairs Research, "Obama's Legacy as President: Depends on Who You Ask," *AP-NORC*, 2017, https://apnorc.org/ projects/obamas-legacy-as-president-depends-on-who-you-ask/.
27. Adam Bonica, Nolan McCarty, Keith T. Poole, and Howard Rosenthal, "Why Hasn't Democracy Slowed Rising Inequality?," *Journal of Economic Perspectives* 27, no. 3 (2013): 103–24.

28. Leslie McCall, Derek Burk, Marie Laperrière, and Jennifer A. Richeson, "Exposure to Rising Inequality Shapes Americans' Opportunity Beliefs and Policy Support," *Proceedings of the National Academy of Sciences* 114, no. 36 (2017): 9593–9598.

29. Matthew Flinders, *Defending Democracy* (Oxford: Oxford University Press, 2012), ix.

30. Mark Stuart, "Whips and Rebels," in *Exploring Parliament*, ed. Cristina Leston-Bandeira and Louise Thompson, 255 (Oxford: Oxford University Press, 2018).

31. For an excellent discussion of these issues in greater depth, see Gerry Stoker's *Why Politics Matters* (Basingstoke: Palgrave Macmillan, 2006).

32. Stephen Welch, *Hyperdemocracy* (Basingstoke: Palgrave Macmillan, 2013), 2.

33. Matthew Flinders and Matt Wood, "When Politics Fails: Hyper-Democracy and Hyper-Depoliticization," *New Political Science* 37, no. 3 (2015): 363–381.

34. Colin Hay and Gerry Stoker, "Revitalising Politics: Have We Lost the Plot?," *Representation* 45, no. 3 (2009): 225–236.

35. Richard Murphy, "Reeves and Starmer: Maintainers of the Status Quo," *Funding the Future*, July 9, 2023, https://www.taxresearch.org.uk/Blog/2023/07/09/reeves-and-starmer-maintainers-of-the-status-quo/.

36. Tom Espiner, "Mortgage Payments Set to Jump By £500 for One Million Households," *BBC News*, July 12, 2023, https://www.bbc.co.uk/news/business-66172954; Larry Elliott, "Risk of UK Recession at Next General Election Is 60 Percent, Says Thinktank," *The Guardian*, August 9, 2023, https://www.theguardian.com/business/2023/aug/09/risk-of-uk-recession-at-next-general-election-is-60-says-thinktank.

37. The Sun, "Rishi Sunak Must Bite the Bullet and Derail Woke HS2—Billions Could Be Saved By Investing in More Immediate Issues," *The Sun*, September 26, 2023, https://www.thesun.co.uk/news/24157181/rishi-sunak-derail-woke-hs2-billions-could-saved/; Sky News, "Rishi Sunak Attacks 'Hare-Brained' Traffic Schemes and Vows to 'Slam Brakes on the War on Motorists,'" *Sky News*, September 30, 2023, https://news.sky.com/story/rishi-sunak-attacks-hare-brained-traffic-schemes-and-vows-to-slam-brakes-on-the-war-on-motorists-12972941.

38. Shanto Iyengar, Gaurav Sood, and Yphtach Lelkes, "Affect, Not Ideology: A Social Identity Perspective on Polarization," *Public Opinion Quarterly* 76, no. 3 (2012): 405–431.

39. Michael Dimock and Richard Wike, "America Is Exceptional in Its Political Divide," *Pew Trusts Magazine*, March 29, 2021, https://www.pewtrusts.org/en/trust/archive/winter-2021/america-is-exceptional-in-its-political-divide.

40. Wendy Wang, "Marriages Between Democrats and Republicans Are Extremely Rare," *Institute for Family Studies*, November 3, 2020, https://ifstudies.org/blog/marriages-between-democrats-and-republicans-are-extremely-rare.

41. Jeremy A. Frimer and Linda J. Skitka, "Are Politically Diverse Thanksgiving Dinners Shorter Than Politically Uniform Ones?" *PLoS One* 15, no. 10 (2010), e0239988, doi: 10.1371/journal.pone.0239988.

42. Katarzyna Jasko, Gary LaFree, James Piazza, and Michael H. Becker, "A Comparison of Political Violence By Left-Wing, Right-Wing, and Islamist Extremists in the United States and the World," *Proceedings of the National Academy of Sciences* 119, no. 30 (2022): e2122593119, doi: 10.1073/pnas.2122593119.

43. Lisa Janssen, "Sweet Victory, Bitter Defeat: The Amplifying Effects of Affective and Perceived Ideological Polarization on the Winner–Loser Gap in Political Support," *European Journal of Political Research* (2023), doi.org/10.1111/1475-6765.12625.

44. Associated Press-NORC Center for Public Affairs Research, "Obama's Legacy As President: Depends on Who You Ask," *AP-NORC*, 2017, https://apnorc.org/projects/obamas-legacy-as-president-depends-on-who-you-ask/.

45. Geoffrey Evans, "The Continued Significance of Class Voting," *Annual Review of Political Science* 3 (2000): 401–417.

46. Jane Mansbridge, "Rethinking Representation," *American Political Science Review* 97, no. 4 (2003): 515–28.

47. David E. Broockman, "Black Politicians Are More Intrinsically Motivated to Advance Blacks' Interests: A Field Experiment Manipulating Political Incentives," *American Journal of Political Science* 57 (2013): 521–536.

48. In another study, Butler and Broockman find that white legislators appear to respond less to Black constituents than white constituents, suggesting that this "extra" representation offered by Black legislators across district lines might be making up a shortfall. Daniel M. Butler and David E. Broockman, "Do Politicians Racially Discriminate Against Constituents? A Field Experiment on State Legislators," *American Journal of Political Science* 55 (2011): 463–477.

49. Aaron Bastani, Twitter, August 21, 2023, https://twitter.com/AaronBastani/status/1693548269945635290.

50. Stacy Smith, Katherine Pieper, and Sam Wheeler, *Inequality in 1,600 Popular Films: Examining Portrayals of Gender, Race/Ethnicity, LGBTQ+ & Disability from 2007 to 2022*, Annenberg Inclusion Initiative (2023), https://assets.uscannenberg.org/docs/aii-inequality-in-1600-popular-films-20230811.pdf; Kate Beioley, "Law Firms Under Pressure to Make More Women Partners," *Financial Times*, October 30, 2023, https://www.ft.com/content/745499be-3ad6-4c9b-ab62-b8cc6830c315; "The Fashion World Promised More Diversity. Here's What We Found," *New York Times*, March 4, 2021, https://www.nytimes.com/2021/03/04/style/Black-representation-fashion.html.

51. Kimmy Yam, "'Oppenheimer' Draws Debate Over the Absence of Japanese Bombing Victims in the Film," *NBC News*, July 26, 2023, https://www.nbcnews.com/news/asian-america/oppenheimer-draws-debate-absence-japanese-bombing-victims-film-rcna96279.

52. The Guardian, "Whose Life Is It Anyway? Novelists Have Their Say on Cultural Appropriation," *The Guardian*, October 1, 2016, https://www.theguardian.com/books/2016/oct/01/novelists-cultural-appropriation-literature-lionel-shriver.

53. Catherine Rottenberg, "The Rise of Neoliberal Feminism," *Cultural Studies*, 28, no. 3 (2014): 418–437.

54. Rottenberg, "The Rise of Neoliberal Feminism," 420.

55. Dawn Foster, *Lean Out* (London: Repeater Books, 2016).

56. Joseph Rowntree Foundation, "Overall UK Poverty Rates, 2023," https://www.jrf.org.uk/data/overall-uk-poverty-rates (accessed August 19, 2024).

57. Jonathan Cribb, Tom Wernham, and Xiaowei Xu, "Pre-Pandemic Relative Poverty Rate for Children of Lone Parents Almost Double That for Children Living with Two Parents," *Institute for Fiscal Studies*, July 4, 2022, https://ifs.org.uk/articles/pre-pandemic-relative-poverty-rate-children-lone-parents-almost-double-children-living-two; Amanda Sharfman and Pamela Cobb, "Families and Households in the UK: 2022," *Office for National Statistics*, May 18, 2023, https://www.ons.gov.uk/peoplepopulationandcommunity/birthsdeathsandmarriages/families/bulletins/familiesandhouseholds/2022.

58. Foster, *Lean Out*, 47.

59. Charlotte Alter, "The Failure of the Feminist Industrial Complex," *Time Magazine*, June 24, 2022, https://time.com/6190225/feminist-industrial-complex-roe-v-wade/.

60. Anne Phillips and Hans Asenbaum, "The Politics of Presence Revisited," *Democratic Theory*, 10, no. 2 (2023): 80–89.
61. John E. Van Maanen and Edgar H. Schein, "Toward a Theory of Organizational Socialization," in *Research in Organizational Behavior*, ed. Barry M. Staw, 209–264 (Greenwich, CT: JIP Press, 1979).
62. Peter Allen, "Transformative Experiences in Political Life," *Journal of Political Philosophy*, 25, no. 4 (2017): e40–e59, https://doi.org/10.1111/jopp.12131.
63. Christopher J. Kam, *Party Discipline and Parliamentary Politics* (Cambridge: Cambridge University Press, 2009).
64. Mason Blake and V. Scott H. Solberg, "Designing Elite Football Programmes that Produce Quality Athletes and Future Ready Adults: Incorporating Social Emotional Learning and Career Development," *Soccer & Society* 24, no. 6 (2023): 896–911.
65. Chris Harwood, Ashleigh Drew, and Camilla J. Knight, "Parental Stressors in Professional Youth Football Academies: A Qualitative Investigation of Specialising Stage Parents," *Qualitative Research in Sport and Exercise* 2, no. 1 (2010): 39–55.

Chapter 4

1. Michael C. Bender, *Frankly, We Did Win This Election: The Inside Story of How Trump Lost* (New York: Hachette, 2021), 15.
2. Dominic Rushe, "Trump's Tax Cuts Helped Billionaires Pay Less Than the Working Class for First Time," *The Guardian*, October 9, 2019, https://www.theguardian.com/business/2019/oct/09/trump-tax-cuts-helped-billionaires-pay-less.
3. C. K., "Why People Vote Against Their Economic Interests," *The Economist*, June 5, 2018, https://www.economist.com/democracy-in-america/2018/06/05/why-people-vote-against-their-economic-interests.
4. Note that this is different to holding an expectation that one will actually get much out of politics.
5. Katerina Vráblíková, "How Context Matters? Mobilization, Political Opportunity Structures, and Nonelectoral Political Participation in Old and New Democracies," *Comparative Political Studies* 47, no. 2 (2014): 203–229.
6. Jacob Torfing, "Rethinking Path Dependence in Public Policy Research," *Critical Policy Studies* 3, no. 1 (2009): 70–83, at 71.
7. Adrian Kay, "A Critique of the Use of Path Dependency in Policy Studies," *Public Administration* 83, no. 3 (2005): 553–571, at 553.
8. Robert E. Goodin, "Democracy, Preferences and Paternalism," *Policy Sciences* 26, no. 3 (1993): 229–247.
9. Goodin, "Democracy, Preferences, and Paternalism," 232.
10. Patrick Radden Keefe, "The Family That Built an Empire of Pain," *The New Yorker*, October 30, 2017, https://www.newyorker.com/magazine/2017/10/30/the-family-that-built-an-empire-of-pain.
11. Patrick Radden Keefe, *Empire of Pain* (London: Picador, 2021), 315.
12. George Packer, *The Unwinding: Thirty Years of American Decline* (London: Vintage, 2013), 3.
13. Suhana Hussain, Johana Bhuiyan, and Ryan Menezes, "How Uber and Lyft Persuaded California Their Way," November 13, 2020, https://www.latimes.com/business/technology/story/2020-11-13/how-uber-lyft-doordash-won-proposition-22.
14. Lee Drutman, *The Business of America is Lobbying* (Oxford: Oxford University Press, 2015), 23.

15. Drutman, *The Business of America is Lobbying*, 26.
16. Keith Dowding, *It's the Government, Stupid: How Governments Blame Citizens for Their Own Policies* (Bristol: Bristol University Press, 2020), 2.
17. Zizi Papacharissi, "Democracy Online: Civility, Politeness, and the Democratic Potential of Online Political Discussion Groups," *New Media & Society* 6, no. 2 (2004): 259–283.
18. George Saunders, *The Brain-Dead Megaphone* (London: Bloomsbury, 2007), 17.
19. Saunders, *The Brain-Dead Megaphone*, 18.
20. There is actually a book about somebody doing almost exactly this, which I recommend reading. Matt Fitzgerald, *Running the Dream: One Summer Living, Training, and Racing with a Team of World-Class Runners Half My Age* (New York: Pegasus Books, 2020).
21. Valerie Tiberius, *The Reflective Life: Living Wisely With Our Limits* (Oxford: Oxford University Press, 2008), 14.
22. Tiberius, *The Reflective Life*, 14.
23. Daniel Kahneman, *Thinking, fast and slow* (London: Macmillan, 2011).
24. Quassim Cassim, *Self-Knowledge for Humans* (Oxford: Oxford University Press, 2014), vii.
25. Tiberius, *The Reflective Life*, 33.
26. Kazuo Ishiguro, *The Remains of the Day* (London: Faber & Faber, 1989), 255–256.
27. Tiberius also warns that this can work in the opposite direction—somebody could be "overly reflective at the very time she needs to 'be in the moment'" (*The Reflective Life*, 112).
28. Chris McGreal, "Trump Splits Republican Voters as Friends and Family Clash: 'We Don't Speak'," *The Guardian*, October 9, 2019, https://www.theguardian.com/us-news/2019/oct/09/republicans-divided-at-grassroots-over-trump-we-dont-speak.
29. Belinda Luscome, "'It Makes Me Sick With Grief': Trump's Presidency Divided Families. What Happens to Them Now?," *Time Magazine*, January 21, 2021, https://time.com/5931349/trump-divided-families/.
30. Luscombe, "It Makes Me Sick With Grief."
31. Tiberius, *The Reflective Life*, 117.
32. Tiberius, *The Reflective Life*, 75.
33. Graham Smith, *Democratic Innovations* (Cambridge: Cambridge University Press, 2009).
34. Esteban Ortiz-Ospina, "How Do People Across the World Spend Their Time and What Does This Tell Us About Living Conditions?," *Our World in Data*, December 8, 2020, https://ourworldindata.org/time-use-living-conditions.
35. Robert E. Goodin, James Mahmud Rice, Antti Parpo, and Lina Eriksson, *Discretionary Time: A New Measure of Freedom* (Cambridge: Cambridge University Press, 2008).
36. Statista Research Department, "Restaurant Delivery and Takeaway in the United Kingdom—Statistics & Facts," *Statista*, November 24, 2022, https://www.statista.com/topics/4679/food-delivery-and-takeaway-market-in-the-united-kingdom-uk/#topicOverview.
37. Tiberius, *The Reflective Life*, 76.
38. As an aside, I used to collect directly from the restaurant on a regular basis and I bumped into the woman who works the front of house at this Chinese takeaway during the depths of the COVID-19 lockdown in the UK, an occasion on which we exchanged a socially distanced "hello." If I simply used the app for delivery (not collection), this would never have happened as neither of us would have known what the other looked like.

39. Tiberius, *The Reflective Life*, 81.
40. Valerie Tiberius, *What Do You Want Out of Life: A Philosophical Guide to Figuring Out What Matters* (Princeton, NJ: Princeton University Press, 2023), 159.
41. Lea Ypi, "Political Commitment and the Value of Partisanship," *American Political Science Review* 110, no. 3 (2016): 601–613.
42. Tiberius, *The Reflective Life*, 122.

Chapter 5

1. Brian Greene, *The Hidden Reality* (London: Pelican, 2011).
2. Max Tegmark, *Our Mathematical Universe* (London: Penguin, 2014), 138.
3. Harold D. Lasswell, *Politics: Who Gets What, When, How* (New York: Pickle Partners Publishing, 2018).
4. Mark Fisher, *Capitalist Realism: Is There No Alternative?* (London: John Hunt Publishing, 2009).
5. Peter A. Hall, "Policy Paradigms, Social Learning, and the State: The Case of Economic Policymaking in Britain," *Comparative Politics* 25, no. 3 (1993): 275–96.
6. PBS Frontline, "The Financial Crisis", https://www.pbs.org/wgbh/pages/frontline/oral-history/financial-crisis/tags/the-fallout-from-lehman/.
7. As Peter Hall puts it, "For most of the postwar period, British policy was based on a highly coherent system of ideas associated with John Maynard Keynes. Once adapted to the organization of the British financial system, Keynesian ideas were institutionalized into the procedures of the British Treasury and formalized as the "neoclassical synthesis" in many standard texts. They specified what the economic world was like, how it was to be observed, which goals were attainable through policy, and what instruments should be used to attain them. They became the prism through which policymakers saw the economy as well as their own role within it" (Hall, "Policy paradigms," 279).
8. Adam Tooze, *Crashed: How a Decade of Financial Crisis Changed the World* (London: Penguin, 2018), 77–85.
9. BBC News, "Spending Review 2010: Key Points at-a-Glance," October 21, 2010, https://www.bbc.co.uk/news/uk-politics-11569160.
10. Andrew Gamble, "Austerity as Statecraft," *Parliamentary Affairs* 68, no. 1 (2015): 42–57.
11. Mark Blyth, *Austerity: The History of a Bad Idea* (Oxford: Oxford University Press, 2013).
12. Josephine Tucker, *The Austerity Generation: The Impact of a Decade of Cuts on Family Incomes and Child Poverty* (London: Child Poverty Action Group, 2017).
13. John Quiggin, *Zombie Economics: How Dead Ideas Still Walk Among Us* (Princeton, NJ: Princeton University Press, 2010).
14. Now, we can of course argue about what we mean by "positive effect" and in many cases that is a political question and thus one without a definitive answer. But I will make the assumption that things like mass unemployment, large-scale death and destruction, and so on are bad things that we all want to avoid.
15. Colin Crouch, *The Strange Non-Death of Neoliberalism* (Cambridge: Polity, 2011), 1.
16. For more discussion on what has happened to neoliberalism since 2008, see Tom Hunt and Liam Stanley, "From 'There Is No Alternative' to 'Maybe There Are Alternatives': Five Challenges to Economic Orthodoxy After the Crash," *Political Quarterly*, 90, no. 3 (2019): 479–487.

17. Martin Wolf, "Why So Little Has Changed Since the Financial Crash," *Financial Times*, September 4, 2018, https://www.ft.com/content/c85b9792-aad1-11e8-94bd-cba20d67390c.

18. Erik Kain, "Joe Scarborough Says the Sandy Hook Massacre 'Changed Everything," *Mother Jones*, December 17, 2012, https://www.motherjones.com/politics/2012/12/joe-scarborough-sandy-hook-newtown-gun-control/.

19. Megan Slack, "President Obama Speaks on the Shooting in Connecticut," The White House, December 14, 2012, https://obamawhitehouse.archives.gov/blog/2012/12/14/president-obama-speaks-shooting-connecticut.

20. German Lopez, "How the Parkland Shooting Changed America's Gun Debate," *Vox*, December 26, 2018, https://www.vox.com/2018/12/26/18145305/gun-control-violence-parkland-effect-2018.

21. Brandon Griggs and Christina Walker, "In the Year Since Parkland There's Been a School Shooting, on Average, Every 12 Days," *CNN*, February 14, 2019, https://edition.cnn.com/2019/02/14/us/school-shootings-since-parkland-trnd/index.html.

22. Jennifer Mascia, "Every Day Since Parkland, at Least 3 American Kids Have Been Fatally Shot," *The Trace*, February 13, 2020, https://www.thetrace.org/rounds/every-day-since-parkland-at-least-3-american-kids-have-been-fatally-shot/.

23. Hans J. G. Hassell, John Holbein, and Matthew Baldwin, "Mobilize for Our Lives? School Shootings and Democratic Accountability in U.S. Elections," *American Political Science Review* 114, no. 4 (2020): 1375–1385.

24. *The Economist*, "A Greener Bush," *The Economist*, February 13, 2003, https://www.economist.com/leaders/2003/02/13/a-greener-bush.

25. YouGov, "Belief in Climate Change," https://yougov.co.uk/topics/politics/trackers/belief-in-climate-change (accessed August 19, 2024).

26. Matthew Smith, "International Poll: Most Expect to Feel Impact of Climate Change, Many Think It Will Make Us Extinct," *YouGov*, September 15, 2019, https://yougov.co.uk/topics/science/articles-reports/2019/09/15/international-poll-most-expect-feel-impact-climate.

27. Jonathan Safran Foer, *We Are The Weather: Saving the Planet Begins at Breakfast* (London: Hamish Hamilton, 2019), 34.

28. Reiner Grundmann, "Climate Change as a Wicked Social Problem," *Nature Geoscience* 9 (2016): 562–563.

29. Dale Jamieson, *Reason in a Dark Time: Why the Struggle Against Climate Change Failed—and What It Means for Our Future* (Oxford: Oxford University Press, 2014), 63.

30. Naomi Klein, "Let Them Drown: The Violence of Othering in a Warming World," *London Review of Books* 38, no. 11 (2016), https://www.lrb.co.uk/the-paper/v38/n11/naomi-klein/let-them-drown.

31. Irene Blanken, Niels van de Ven, and Marcel Zeelenberg, "A Meta-Analytic Review of Moral Licensing," *Personality and Social Psychology Bulletin* 41, no. 4 (2015): 540–58.

32. Verena Tiefenbeck, Thorsten Staake, Kurt Roth, and Olga Sachs, "For Better or for Worse? Empirical Evidence of Moral Licensing in a Behavioral Energy Conservation Campaign," *Energy Policy* 57 (2013): 160–71.

33. Jamieson, *Reason in a Dark Time*, 72.

34. David Wallace Wells, *The Uninhabitable Earth* (London: Penguin, 2019).

Conclusion

1. Helen Thompson. *Disorder: Hard times in the 21st Century* (Oxford: Oxford University Press, 2022).

2. Adam Tooze, "Welcome to the World of the Polycrisis," *Financial Times*, October 28, 2022, https://www.ft.com/content/498398e7-11b1-494b-9cd3-6d669dc3de33.
3. Jonathan Derbyshire, "Year in a Word: Polycrisis," *Financial Times*, January 1, 2023, https://www.ft.com/content/f6c4f63c-aa71-46f0-a0a7-c2a4c4a3c0f1.
4. Kate Whiting and HyoJin Park, "This Is Why 'Polycrisis' Is a Useful Way of Looking at the World Right Now," *World Economic Forum*, March 7, 2023, https://www.weforum.org/agenda/2023/03/polycrisis-adam-tooze-historian-explains/.
5. Ibid.
6. Tooze, "Welcome to the World of the Polycrisis."
7. David Henig and Daniel M. Knight, "Polycrisis: Prompts for an Emerging Worldview," *Anthropology Today* 39, no. 2 (2023): 3–6.
8. Henrik Vigh, "Crisis and Chronicity: Anthropological Perspectives on Continuous Conflict and Decline," *Ethnos* 73, no. 1 (2008): 5–24.
9. Andrew Daniller, "Americans Take a Dim View of the Nation's Future, Look More Positively at the Past," *Pew Research Center*, April 24, 2023, https://www.pewresearch.org/short-reads/2023/04/24/americans-take-a-dim-view-of-the-nations-future-look-more-positively-at-the-past.
10. Nikhil Venkatesh, "Inefficacy, Pre-emption and Structural Injustice," *Proceedings of the Aristotelian Society* 123, no. 3 (2023), https://doi.org/10.1093/arisoc/aoad014.
11. Andreas Malm, *How to Blow Up a Pipeline* (London: Verso Books, 2021).
12. Jonathan Safran Foer, *We Are The Weather: Saving the Planet Begins at Breakfast* (London: Hamish Hamilton, 2019), 23.
13. Benjamin Kunkel, "The Amazon Burning," *London Review of Books*, 41, no. 17 (2019), https://www.lrb.co.uk/the-paper/v41/n17/benjamin-kunkel/short-cuts.
14. David Wallace Wells, *The Uninhabitable Earth* (London: Penguin, 2019), 283.
15. Dan Barry and Sheera Frenkel, "'Be There. Will Be Wild!': Trump All But Circled the Date," *New York Times*, January 6, 2021, https://www.nytimes.com/2021/01/06/us/politics/capitol-mob-trump-supporters.html.
16. Daniel Trotta, Gabriella Borter, and Jonathan Allen, "Woman Killed in Siege of U.S. Capitol Was Veteran Who Embraced Conspiracy Theories," Reuters, January 7, 2021, https://www.reuters.com/article/uk-usa-election-death-idUKKBN29C2NX.
17. Ibid.
18. Lois Beckett and Vivian Ho, "'She Was Deep Into It': Ashli Babbitt, Killed in Capitol Riot, Was Devoted Conspiracy Theorist," *The Guardian*, January 9, 2021, https://www.theguardian.com/us-news/2021/jan/09/ashli-babbitt-capitol-mob-trump-qanon-conspiracy-theory.
19. Rosie Frost, "Just Stop Oil: Climate Activists Explain Why They Are Attacking Artwork," *EuroNews.Green*, July 9, 2022, https://www.euronews.com/green/2022/07/09/just-stop-oil-climate-activists-explain-why-they-are-gluing-themselves-to-art.
20. Mattias Wahlström, Piotr Kocyba, Michiel De Vydt, and Joost de Moor, eds., *Protest for a Future: Composition, Mobilization and Motives of the Participants in Fridays For Future Climate Protests on 15 March, 2019 in 13 European Cities*, Institut für Protest- und Bewegungsforschung, 2019, eprints.keele.ac.uk/6571/; Felix Noth and Lena Tonzer, "Understanding Climate Activism: Who Participates in Climate Marches Such as 'Fridays for Future' and What Can We Learn from It?," *Energy Research & Social Science* 84 (2022): 102360; https://doi.org/10.1016/j.erss.2021.102360.
21. Joshi Shashank, "The War in Ukraine May Be Heading for Stalemate," *The Economist*, November 13, 2023, https://www.economist.com/the-world-ahead/2023/11/13/the-war-in-ukraine-may-be-heading-for-stalemate.
22. Courtney Kube, Carol E. Lee, and Kristen Welker, "U.S., European Officials Broach Topic of Peace Negotiations with Ukraine, Sources Say," *NBC News*,

November 3, 2023, https://www.nbcnews.com/news/world/us-european-officials-broach-topic-peace-negotiations-ukraine-sources-rcna123628.

23. Jaroslav Lukiv, "Ukraine War: Zelensky Says Israel-Gaza Conflict Taking Focus Away from Fighting," BBC News, November 4, 2023,https://www.bbc.co.uk/news/world-europe-67321777.

24. Aditya Chakrabortty, "The Westminster Panto Is in Full Swing: But There Are Real Dangers Waiting in the Wings," *The Guardian*, November 9, 2023, https://www.theguardian.com/commentisfree/2023/nov/09/westminster-war-economic-breakdown-climate-crisis-end-of-history-politicians.

25. Liam Stanley, *Britain Alone* (Manchester: Manchester University Press, 2022), 35.

26. Henig and Knight, "Polycrisis", 6.

27. David Graeber, *The Utopia of Rules* (New York: Melville House), 89.

Index

gender quotas and increasing diversity
of 71–75
impact of changes in 76
increasing diversity of 74–75
logic of representation 86–87
positive story about 69
race 84
surrogate representation 84
see also representative democracy
Purdue Pharma 100
Oxycontin and 100
Sackler family and 100

representative democracy
complexity of decision-making
processes 80
depoliticization and 81–82
frustrations of 80, 153–154
hyper-democracy and 81–82
path dependency and 97–98
repoliticization 82
see also presence
Rooney, Sally 28–29
Rottenberg, Catherine 86–87

Saunders, George:
'Megaphone Guy' 103–104
Smith, Zadie 30
social class 29–30
accent 31–32
fitting in 32
social media:

climate change and 155–156
democratic potential of 103–104
political voice and 103–104
polycrisis and 155–156
Starmer, Keir 16
political skill of 56–57
Stauffer, Katelyn E. 75–76

Tegmark, Max 120–122
Thompson, Helen 149
Tiberius, Valerie 107
reflection and the good life 107, 118
Tooze, Adam 4–5, 149–151
Trump, Donald 10, 42, 69–70, 82, 93–94,
130–158
conflict within families as a result of
113–114
'Front Row Joes' 93–94, 118
January 6 2021 and 158–159

values:
changes in what we value 105–106
conflict in our values 107, 111
endorsing what we value after
reflection 159
inappropriate values 94–111
political action and 154

Wallace, David Foster 35, 97
woke:
critiques of 33–34, 82, 89
Douglas Murray 33–34